BEYOND THE BOTTOM LINE

BEYOND THE BOTTOM LINE

How to Do More

with Less in

Nonprofit and

Public Organizations

Martin W. Sandler

Deborah A. Hudson

With Carol Weiss and Neil deGuzmán

New York   Oxford

Oxford University Press

1998

Oxford University Press

Oxford   New York
Athens   Auckland   Bangkok   Bogota   Bombay
Buenos Aires   Calcutta   Cape Town   Dar es Salaam
Delhi   Florence   Hong Kong   Istanbul   Karachi
Kuala Lumpur   Madras   Madrid   Melbourne
Mexico City   Nairobi   Paris   Singapore
Taipei   Tokyo   Toronto   Warsaw

and associated companies in
Berlin   Ibadan

Copyright © 1998 by Oxford University Press, Inc.

Published by Oxford University Press, Inc.
198 Madison Avenue, New York, New York 10016

Oxford is a registered trademark of Oxford University Press

Library of Congress Cataloging-in-Publication Data
Sandler, Martin W.
Beyond the bottom line : how to do more with less
in nonprofit and public organizations /
Martin W. Sandler and Deborah A. Hudson.
p. cm.
ISBN 0-19-511612-7
1. Administrative agencies—United States—Management.
2. Nonprofit organizations—United States—Management.
I. Hudson, Deborah A.   II. Title.
JK421.S27 1998
658'.048—DC21   97-14584

9 8 7 6 5 4 3 2 1

Printed in the United States of America
on acid-free paper

FOREWORD

Excellence in public and nonprofit organizations. To many it might seem a contradiction in terms. Yet if there is one thing above all else that I learned from my personal information and from this book it is that business corporations have no corner on transforming themselves into efficiently managed, results-oriented, customer-driven organizations. The nonprofits and public agencies cited are as bold and daring as those with whom I have visited and consulted. They are challenging the outdated assumptions about the hide-bound, slow, and unresponsive organizations that common knowledge tells us predominate outside the innovative, fast-moving business world.

Typical of the organizations whose strategies for effectiveness are contained throughout this book is a relatively little-known government agency in Northumberland County, Pennsylvania. During a consolidation, Mike Breslin, who was in charge of juvenile justice, was given the added responsibility of directing mental health and mental retardation services. Instead of resisting the apparent downsizing, he used his expanded role to reengineer these departments into what became the Children's Clinic.

As Breslin explains, the old way of delivering services was complex, costly, and time consuming—and it often exacerbated the very problems it was meant to solve. When a kid got in trouble in the courts or at school, a case worker would do an assessment and pass him to the "appropriate" agency. There they did another assessment and they might draw up a treatment program, but they also might decide it was *not* their problem and refer the kid to yet another agency where a third assessment was done. It often happened that it took more than a month to get actual help to a family. "By that time," says Breslin, "the immediate crisis was over, and the family, more often than not, had lost hope or interest."

So Breslin put together a customer-driven team process for getting help to troubled kids and their families as quickly and effectively as possible. The Children's Clinic smashes ages-old bureaucratic barriers by addressing the simple question: "What does this child and family need?" rather than "What do we have to offer?" or "What funds does a particular department have?" The Clinic addresses its purpose from the customer's point of view, not from the internal bureaucratic perspective of many organizations.

There's no new money, no new offices, no fancy signs at the Children's Clinic. It's really just a meeting. Every Wednesday afternoon, representatives from every agency in the County's Human Services Department sit down at one table with the child in question and his or her family and work out a treatment plan. No one leaves the table until a realistic plan for helping the youngster is devised and the customers have agreed to the plan. Representatives of the various agencies commit resources on the spot.

Mike Breslin is only one of dozens of skilled and committed nonprofit and public agency managers whose approaches and strategies are collected in this book. The authors are no think tank theorists. They show genuine respect for the insight of managers who have worked to keep a production schedule or have laid awake worrying about how to turn around an unproductive worker. They acknowledge the tough realities of managing and they refuse to sacrifice the complexities of the real world to the seductive simplicity of theory. They offer no magic cures, no quick and painless "fixes" for the persistent challenges of nonprofit and public organizations. For me, that is the highest possible recommendation for this book. It is infused with the experiences of managers in the trenches. It is a hands-on catalog of the nuts and bolts strategies that these managers employ to transform their organizations, particularly at a time when they are being asked to do much more with much less.

These people and organizations offer proof that nonprofits and public agencies can not only supply the services they were created to deliver, but can do so in a manner that exceeds all of our expectations. Indeed, the central thesis of this book is not that it can be done, but that it is *being* done. The countless approaches and strategies cited provide nothing less than a blueprint for transforming an organization through management excellence, no matter what the sector of operation.

James A. Champy

PREFACE

Look at the shelves in the management section of any bookstore. Where are the books about the top-performing government agencies or nonprofit organizations? Is there really that little to say about the art and science of management outside of the corporate world? Or are for-profit businesses that much better managed? Should performance be graded on a curve with business at the top of the class, nonprofits as underachievers, and government bringing up the rear?

These questions started us on a five-year journey that led to this book. In 1988 Martin Sandler and his partner, Carol Weiss, approached Tom Peters, co-author of *In Search of Excellence* and timeless advocate of skilled and visionary management, with a proposal to create an hour-long television program profiling outstanding public service organizations. Deborah Hudson came to the project as associate producer. In 1989 that program, "Excellence in the Public Sector with Tom Peters," was broadcast by the Public Broadcasting System to wide acclaim. As a result, we received dozens of requests to speak to civic, business, and administrative groups. Obviously the program had touched a nerve, and together we decided to write a book that could examine many more effective public and nonprofit organizations and dig deeper into the strategies and approaches that led to their success.

We approach our task as citizens—not as management theorists. We are motivated by our stake in good government and a strong nonprofit sector and by our belief that providing concrete lessons from the best in these sectors is the most effective way to help those who work for the public good. We have no organizational model to follow or patented nostrum to cure every ill. Our work plan can be summed up by Alex Haley's dictum, "Find the good and praise it." Our careers have given us skills as interviewers and observers. Martin Sandler is the author of more than twenty books. Deborah Hudson is a researcher, writer, and film producer and has worked on several projects for The Tom Peters Group. Carol Weiss is an organizational consultant with years of experience working with both public- and private-sector organizations.

We began this book by defining our mission: to find the best-managed nonprofit and government agencies, to analyze them and pinpoint the specific strategies that make them a success, and to communicate these strategies in a manner that will enable organizations everywhere to learn from the best. Next, we did our homework. We read widely. We contacted leaders of professional associations; academics; management consultants; heads of foundations, private- and public-sector executives; and other experts with special knowledge of public- and independent-sector organizations. We asked them which organizations they considered most effective.

We contacted candidate organizations and asked questions and more questions—and even more after that. Out of this process we developed a roster of forty-five finalists, not "the best of the best" but a representative cross-section of top-performing organizations with a range of effective management strategies that were readily adaptable to other organizations. The list included federal, state, and local government as well as nonprofit organizations from every region of the country, large organizations and small, well known and obscure.

Then we visited each finalist on site. We attended meetings, watched operations, shadowed executives, ate in the company cafeteria (even when the "company" was a prison), and interviewed top executives, managers, employees, and customers. After more than a year on the road, we reduced our roster to twenty-four organizations. Then came the hard work of pinpointing the management strategies, approaches, and innovations that contribute to these organizations' success. Finally, we sat down to communicate what we'd discovered. It is our hope that we conveyed what we have found in a manner worthy of those who have made excellence in the public service a reality.

ACKNOWLEDGMENTS

If we've succeeded in producing the book we set out to write, it will be thanks to the advice and inspiration of many talented people. We owe a deep debt of gratitude to everyone mentioned in the book. We only hope that this book conveys a sufficient sense of their commitment to public service, their skills, and their ability to do tough jobs knowing everything they do is on public display and open to public debate. We are particularly grateful to Ellen Schall, Sandy Stiner Lowe, Rod Collins, and Sandra Hale, who, beyond detailing stories of their own organizations, helped us further by sharing their insights into managing effectively in any public service organization. There were those behind the scenes to whom we are also indebted. First we must thank Tom Peters, who set us on our way almost ten years ago and then left us alone to make our own discoveries. His name opened doors for us, and his sharp intelligence and unrelenting energy always inspired us. We are most grateful to Jim Champy for providing the foreword to the book. We wish to thank Bill Delaney of the U.S. Forest Service for answering our many questions and pointing us in the right direction. We also wish to acknowledge the special help we received from Phoenix's Mark Hughes, the GAO's Emily Heller, and the USGS's Pete Bermel. Finally we acknowledge the very special support we received from the following individuals: Robert Downing, William O. Bailey, Lois Baldwin, Jack Butler, Paul DiMaura, Hal A. Levine, Fritz Mueller, Jr., and Peter Wetherbee.

CONTENTS

BEYOND THE BOTTOM LINE

INTRODUCTION

This book looks beyond the realm of business for lessons in the art and science of management. In the last five years, we have developed some two dozen detailed case studies of top-performing public and nonprofit organizations, from high-profile giants like the Girl Scouts of the USA to little-known pioneers like the Children's Clinic of Northumberland County, Pennsylvania. We've put these organizations under the microscope, studying them to understand the specific techniques and strategies and approaches that put these organizations ahead of the pack. At every turn, our primary interest was to distill practical lessons that could be taken from one context and used in other organizational settings by other managers.

There is no prescription or blueprint for achieving excellence as a manager. The only "secret of success" is that it demands constant effort on every front. If any aspect is neglected, the entire effort to achieve excellence is compromised. That, in a nutshell, is the challenge of managing. Each manager knows her own situation best. Each reader will find some observations or lessons more useful than others. What works in one setting can be inappropriate for the organization across the street. What works in March may fail in May. But if you are committed to fundamental improvements in your organizations, these are practical, proven strategies that can help your whole organization work smarter and better.

Much has been written about the heroic struggles of corporate managers to meet the challenge of managing in today's turbulent and rapidly changing economy. Many assume that managing public agencies and nonprofits is somehow sailing in smoother waters, away from the shocks of the market. We disagree strongly. While

3

managers in government and nonprofits may be sheltered from the market, they are exposed to more rigorous and unrelenting scrutiny and are often caught in the crossfire of conflicting constituencies. The men and women we met during our research constantly battle constraints that would weaken the resolve of many of their counterparts in the business world. And they do their work during a time of extraordinary upheaval in their arena of operations. As former chief Neil Behan of the Baltimore County police told us, "If you're looking for a nice, simple place to manage in, forget it; it's gone. If you don't understand this and you keep looking for order, you're not going to be able to manage."

Although we group nonprofit and government agencies together throughout the book, there are a few important differences in the ways managers are limited and challenged in each area.

The Government Sector

What makes a top-performing organization? It's tough to answer that question with regard to government agencies, for two reasons. First, whether government is operating well or not is a matter of point of view. When we want a new public road to run by our property, we want it built without long deliberation beforehand. But when federal or state officials want to build a prison in our county, we want lots of meetings and hearings. Second, government was created to run *less* efficiently than either businesses or nonprofits. "The governments of the United States," writes political scientist James Q. Wilson in his book, *Bureaucracy*, "were not designed to be efficient or powerful, but to be tolerable and malleable." Adds Wilson, "All complex organizations display bureaucratic problems of confusion, red tape, and the avoidance of responsibility. Those problems are much greater in government bureaucracies because government itself is the institutionalization of confusion (arising out of the need to moderate competing demands); of red tape (arising out of the needs to satisfy demands that cannot be moderated); and of avoided responsibility (arising out of the desire to retain power by minimizing criticism)." Any effort to make government more efficient must take the following qualities into account.

Vague and ambiguous goals.   Government organizations are often charged with meeting nebulous goals—for instance, "to develop urban communities" or "to provide quality education" or "to promote and regulate air transportation." These goals are difficult to translate into operational objectives and precise courses of action, and developing measures of performance or progress is tough indeed.

Multiple constituencies.   Government agencies often serve several constituencies, which frequently have conflicting agendas and make competing demands on the agency mandated to serve them. The U.S. Forest Service, for example, is mandated to serve "the land and the people." But how does it mediate the conflicting interests of groups such as loggers, environmentalists, ranchers, hunters, and vacationers?

Budget processes.   Government budget processes were designed as a check against misappropriation and fraud, but they have become so demanding that managers spend an inordinate amount of time on tasks that contribute nothing toward the organization's productivity.

Staffing procedures.   Government personnel systems, established to ensure fairness and opportunity, have come to pose a serious challenge to efficiency. Federal employees, for instance, are ranked in narrowly defined wage and task categories that often have little to do with an individual's abilities or achievements. Government staffing procedures leave administrators with fewer powers to hire, fire, transfer, promote, or demote than their nonprofit-sector counterparts possess.

Political context.   An enormous number of government executives move in and out of their offices based on election results. American presidents now control approximately 1,500 top-level managerial appointments. Most governors and mayors have similar powers. In the federal government, political appointees serve in their positions for an average of approximately eighteen months. That's hardly enough time for even the most able managers to learn the ropes. Nor is it sufficient time to devise and implement sensible programs or see them through to completion.

The Nonprofit Sector

If there are magicians in this book, they are the dedicated managers of nonprofits who take a $100 contribution and turn it into $600 worth of meals for the homeless or a three–act marionette play. They are networkers, salespeople, and partnership builders of the first order, and they have much to teach any manager. Yet there still exists a belief that a manager can learn nothing from "fuzzy-thinking idealists" and "blue-haired ladies" out to save the world. Three of the most important (and inhibiting) of these misconceptions about the nonprofit sector are labeled by Richard Steckel, former executive director of the Children's Museum of Denver, as "the three big lies":

> *"Nonprofit means no profit"*—the first big lie. Nonprofit simply means that the excess of revenues over expenses go back into the organization and are not distributed outside the organization. Folks in the nonprofit sector have been telling

themselves for years that nonprofits can't make a profit. That's not true. Nonprofits have to understand the importance of earning as much income as they can. Nonprofits can't keep asking people for money over and over and over again.

"Nonprofit organizations deserve your support"—the second big lie. No one deserves anyone's support because they are what they are. Organizations only deserve support when they do something that meets a need. The nonprofit, for example, receives something of value (cash, in-kind services, volunteers, etc.) and the contributors receive something of value (a business edge, participation in a cause they believe in, warm fuzzies). When people start believing that as a nonprofit organization they automatically deserve community support they've bought the second big lie and begin to sink into a mentality that says "feed me, feed me, feed me," and without obligation to provide quality service.

"Nonprofit organizations can afford to be mediocre"—the third big lie. How many times have you heard a nonprofit manager say, "We have to put up with the mediocre receptionist because we can't afford to pay a salary to attract a qualified employee?" Mediocrity can run deep in nonprofit organizations because nonprofits don't face the plain fact that they are a business like any other business. Just like in the retail food industry, there are good businesses and bad businesses among the nonprofits. Unfortunately, nonprofits' batting average is not as high as our brethren in the profit sector.

The Plan of This Book

The body of this book is divided into two sections: competencies and challenges. Competencies are the stuff of most management books, the practical strategies that make the organizations we studied peak performers. The challenges are the issues that guide organizational life. To use a metaphor, challenges are the compass readings and the charts by which a successful organization set its courses, steers itself, and keeps everyone sailing in the same direction. The competencies are the skills of seamanship that keep the organizational vessel afloat and in top working order.

Part I has three chapters, which include over seventy-five separate applications.

Chapter 1, "The Challenge of Mission," reviews the importance of a clear mission. All the government agencies and nonprofits we studied know that mission is the cornerstone of their organization. They take great pains to define their mission properly. They make sure that everyone clearly understands it, and they stick to it religiously.

Chapter 2, "The Challenge of Change," examines the implications of change. The organizations we cite know that change is ever-present and that in order to operate effectively they must not only commit to change but must develop approaches and strategies to make change an intrinsic part of their organizational culture.

Chapter 3, "The Challenge of Managing for Results," looks at the importance of setting and working toward achievable goals. Each of the best nonprofit and public organizations understands that outcomes are more important than process. They plan, set goals, hold everyone accountable, and they continually measure the performance of both individuals and the organization itself.

In Part II there are seven chapters, which include over two hundred readily adaptable strategies.

Chapter 4, "Serving the Customer," explores the crucial role played by the customer or constituent. All these organizations understand that they exist first and foremost to serve their customers. They have developed strategies to identify and listen to the customer and to constantly assess and reassess their priorities.

Chapter 5, "Selling the Product," stresses the value of competitive marketing. Many of our vanguard organizations aggressively market and sell their products and services.

Chapter 6, "Forming Effective Partnerships," adresses the need for cooperative sharing of ideas and resources. Most of the organizations we studied leverage resources through partnerships. By joining forces with outside partners, they are able to bring in new financial and human resources and fresh ideas.

Chapter 7, "Creating a Climate for Innovation," celebrates the power of creative thinking. The best government agencies and nonprofits we studied make a science of constant innovation. They solicit new ideas from everyone. They recognize and reward contributors for ideas that work, and they encourage everyone to examine other organizations for good ideas to "swipe."

Chapter 8, "Sharing the Power," looks at the delegation of responsibility. All of the organizations we studied demonstrate that giving decision-making power to those closest to the action is one of the most direct routes to organizational effectiveness.

Chapter 9, "Valuing People," recognizes the human equation. All of the government agencies and nonprofits studied here are characterized by the value they assign to their people, the trust they place in them, and the respect they show them. All invest heavily in training people and celebrating their accomplishments.

Chapter 10, "Communicating Effectively," stresses the development and nurturing of communications skills and strategies. The government agencies and nonprofits we examined understand that in today's decentralized organization, characterized by autonomous teams, communication is the glue that holds the structure together.

We believe that every manager will find something of real value in the following pages—lessons and strategies that can be applied to an organization. It is our fervent hope that this book will also expand public understanding of the nature of managing government and nonprofit organizations, that it will aid in developing an appreciation of what is being accomplished by dedicated, hard-working public servants, and that it will help move citizens beyond the knee-jerk criticism that has become so prevalent in recent years.

PART I

CHALLENGES

The people we met in our travels were powerful, competent, daring
men and women involved in the management of large and complex
organizations. They were eager to discuss their achievements and
accomplishments, the subtleties of the art and science of management. But over time, we noticed that they talked more about interesting problems than about clever solutions. We spent many hours
listening to them describe how the problems arose, how people in the
organization became aware of them, how the problems affected the
organization, and how they challenged old thinking and created new
opportunities. These managers took time to celebrate their triumphs,
but they were always looking ahead to the next puzzle.

We came to realize that these leaders were really telling us to look
beyond answers. They were saying that effective organizations are
built of more than a pile of strategies. They were calling our attention
to the quicksilver nature of organizational life and the fact that healthy
organizations are the products not just of answers, but of the willingness and the discipline to pose tough questions.

We were drawn up short. Our self-appointed task was to observe
and analyze successful organizations and their managers and pass
along our findings. We were in the midst of compiling an impressive
roster of tools and techniques to address organizational problems—
and now we realized that our subjects were telling us to look beyond
strategies to the dilemmas themselves. It is the dilemmas that pull a
team together, that fuel growth and productivity, that engage the
best in each employee. There are some dilemmas—or challenges—
that can never be solved or overcome. The questions Why are we
here? Why do we do things the way we do? Where are we headed?
Are we making progress? How can we tell? need to be addressed

again and again by people at every level of the organization. These questions are never meant to be answered fully; their function is to stimulate new responses and to create new options.

Most important, they provide the discipline that transforms the commitment to serve into achievement.

Why are we here?   The organization's mission is always open to question from all employees and stakeholders. Questions keep it vivid and alive, help it keep pace with changing realities, and make it worthy of attention and support.

What's going on here?   Why are we doing things the way we do? Organizations must be committed to constant change, and not merely as an abstract principle. They must question their environment and status daily in order to keep up.

Where are we headed?   Are we making progress? In order to be accountable to stakeholders for accomplishing their mission, organizations must *manage for results*. Careful planning and measurement, constant monitoring of quality, and continual debate over the nature of indicators keep organizations focused on goals and tasks.

1

THE CHALLENGE
OF MISSION

How are we doing? Businesses answer that question by looking at the balance sheet, at cash register receipts, at the closing value of their stock. Nonprofits and government organizations look at mission.

Mission is such a strong cohesive force that the corporate world has adopted the mission statement with a vengeance—and with mixed results. Some organizations have found that this new clarity of purpose has boosted morale and productivity. Others have created new dissension in the ranks by making a poorly designed mission statement the focus of a booster campaign, complete with posters and pins.

Mission is the bedrock of the organizations we studied. These top performers managed through their mission, by their mission, and, above all, for their mission. Everyone at every level of these organizations is aware of the mission, understands it, and has a stake in it. More than any other single factor, mission connects employees and their values to the organization and its task. Mission is the yardstick by which priorities are established. In an economic downturn or funding crisis, when two opportunities present themselves and only one can be seized, when budgets are allocated, then mission sets the measure for the debate and defines the terms in which that debate is conducted.

Despite its ability to focus and clarify issues, there's nothing simple about mission. It may be the most demanding of any challenge an organization faces. It provides stability, so it cannot alter with the fashions of the season. Yet it cannot be a closed book: it must be able to accommodate the shocks of change, and each new organizational generation must make the mission its own. It must be open to question, comment, discussion, and debate from any employee, customer, or stakeholder.

Outside realities can force a reexamination of mission. In the 1980s, when the Girl Scouts were losing members at a troubling clip, there was talk of changing the mission, of opening membership to boys. The March of Dimes, founded to fight polio, outlived its original mandate when the Salk and Sabine vaccines virtually eradicated that disease, and so the organization re-directed its fundraising, education, and research efforts and expanded its mission to include the fight against all childhood diseases and defects.

When is it right to change a mission? When is change necessary for survival and when will it damage the organization? The Girl Scouts, who today have more members than ever before, achieved success by sticking to the original mission of serving girls and updating the organization's concept of just who the girls are. For organizations like the March of Dimes or New York City's Department of Juvenile Justice, expanding the mission has been the key to survival and renewal.

In this chapter, we outline how organizations use the challenge of mission to navigate the rough waters of change, to guide their efforts and prioritize their tasks, and to encourage their people to attain new levels of performance.

Tie Everything to the Mission

The organization we know that best embodies the challenge of mission—and the ways it tempers and tests an organization—is not a big blue blood like the Salvation Army. It is a small scrapper called the National Theatre Workshop of the Handicapped (NTWH).

As you take the elevator up to NTWH's main facilities on the fifth floor of a Manhattan office building, you become suddenly conscious of the chorus of voices belting out a musical number. You step off the elevator and there they are in the studio in front of you—intense, animated, and obviously very talented. Then it hits you. Everyone on stage is either blind, in a wheelchair, or on crutches.

NTWH, an organization founded in 1977 by Jesuit brother Rick Curry, a tall, handsome, charismatic Steve Martin look-alike, was created to provide professional training in the performing arts for physically disabled adults. Curry's understanding of the needs of the disabled comes naturally, since he was born with one arm. Not that that has slowed him down. A man of boundless energy, Curry has devoted more than twenty years to building an organization designed to meet the needs of a hitherto neglected segment of the population.

"Disabled people," explains Brother Rick, "are benignly ignored, which is worse than being confronted. We're very talented human beings; arts are our heritage. It makes far more sense objectively to train a disabled person in the arts than in sports, for example, because the imagination has not been crippled. I admire a skier who is also disabled but that is an able-bodied expectation. As an arts group developing a new culture, our horizons are unlimited."

The idea for NTWH came to Curry when, while pursuing a doctoral degree at New York University, he was asked to conduct a study for the Department of Health, Education, and Welfare. "At that time," says Brother Rick, "the O'Neil Theatre Center housed the National Theatre of the Deaf and HEW wanted to explore ways in which the O'Neil could be used for other disabled groups. I did the study and concluded that there was an enormous need for a theatre for all disabled people but that it wouldn't work in conjunction with the National Theatre of the Deaf. A theatre for the disabled needed its own identity and its own life and, as my doctoral dissertation, I outlined what I thought it should be. Then I threw a cocktail party where I announced that I was going to form NTWH with a curriculum and a faculty and we raised $5,000 at that party. I took that money, rented a loft, had letterhead printed and got started."

Today, NTWH is a highly respected, professional acting school with an array of courses and an ambitious repertory season. NTWH's overall program includes:

- A curriculum including acting, play writing, directing, voice and movement, and singing.
- Workshops that bring in working professionals to conduct short-term classes on a broad range of topics relating to the theater.
- A repertory company that presents musical and dramatic performances throughout the year in venues across the country.
- A short works festival that solicits theatrical pieces dealing with themes relating to the disabled. Winning entries are performed by the student body.
- An annual gala performance staged as a benefit at an annual celebration of the year's progress.
- A puppet theater for children and adults.
- A residential theater in Belfast, Maine.

To date, more than six hundred students at NTWH have received instruction in some aspect of the performing arts. A slowly increasing number have appeared in films, on television, and on the professional stage. High on the list of NTWH's priorities is developing a body of works examining the experiences of the disabled. Says

Brother Rick, "When you can tell a story about how a blind person operates, how an orthopedically disabled person operates, how people with different disabilities relate to each other, someone in the audience will say, 'Oh, I never thought of that before.' That's great. That's what our organization is all about."

"We're unique," says NTWH's board chairman, Rob Sennott. "We're the only organization of our kind in the world. Our philosophy is to celebrate disability, not to ignore it. Everything we do is related to that mission. It's reflected in our administrative structure and in our ideology. We're attempting not just to reach a community but to create a specific community of the disabled and to empower it until it begins to guide us. And it's happening."

Brother Rick Curry emphasizes that NTWH's unique mission is fundamental to its success. "We're aware of our mission every day. And that leads to an all-consuming fidelity to the program. Every day you have to come in and take care of the baby. We're advocates for a very specific population that's far from united. It's not as if we were responding to a felt need. We're creating that need. In fact, we're developing the literature as we go along. And don't forget, arts are not high on the priorities of Americans the way movies and sports are. Put all of these things together and you have a great fragility. And that's why we're fanatic about our mission. If we weren't, we'd never make it."

Stewards of the Mission

The National Theatre Workshop of the Handicapped owes a considerable part of its success to its board of directors. We asked board chairman Rob Sennott to list what he regards as the four most important characteristics of an effective board:

1. You must have people who see themselves as stewards of the organization's mission, individuals who will do everything they can to see that the mission is fulfilled.
2. You have to include people with specific skills that relate to the organization's mission. You should try to include someone who is familiar with the press and/or public relations, a lawyer, and an accountant or someone who knows how to put together a balance sheet.
3. You must have people who can get along well with the organization's director and staff.
4. You must have rainmakers—people who have connections with important potential donors to the organization and people who can use their connections to "sell" the organization's mission. And you need people who have previous successful experience in fundraising.

Use the Mission to Set Priorities

Many of the agencies and corporations we studied are large and complex organizations charged with carrying out a myriad of tasks. For them, one of the challenges of mission is translating it into operational priorities.

We often think about the federal bureaucracy as if it were one giant, gray mass. But government agencies are as different from one another as makes and models of cars. The Pentagon might be a Cadillac with power, performance, and lots of expensive extras. The Forest Service is a four-wheel-drive Jeep. Represented by a stripped-down Chevy, with a few dings but with a police engine under its hood, is the Centers for Disease Control and Prevention (CDC). It doesn't look for or get many admiring glances. It just covers the miles, doing the job of collecting statistics and coordinating local public health efforts. But every once in a while it pulls out into the fast lane and captures the public's attention with its speed and performance.

The Centers for Disease Control and Prevention began in 1942 under the name of the Office of Malaria Control in War Areas. Because malaria was endemic to the South, the organization was located in Atlanta. Within three years, the identification and prevention of dengue, typhus, and yellow fever were added to its mission, and in 1945 a tropical diseases laboratory was established under its control to help diagnose exotic infections that some thought might be brought into the United States by servicemen returning from World War II. In 1946, a career public health officer, Dr. Joseph Mountin, proposed that the organization become an activist partner with the research-oriented National Institutes of Health. In his proposal, some thirty years ahead of Tom Peters and Bob Waterman, Mountin stated the need for "a center of excellence," and his proposal was given form in what became the Communicable Disease Center, which we now know as the Centers for Disease Control and Prevention.

Driven by an all-embracing mission "to improve the quality of life for all Americans by preventing unnecessary disease, disability, and premature death and by promoting healthy lifestyles," the CDC employs administrators, scientists, computer specialists, chemists, environmental engineers, epidemiologists, lab technicians, microbiologists, pharmacologists, analysts, physicians, statisticians, and toxicologists, scattered throughout the United States and abroad. Former director Dr. William Roper was able to tie all these diverse projects, programs, and professionals together by establishing priorities around a common mission. "There are many ideas and opportunities that come along for an organization like

CDC," says Roper. "Focusing energy and attention on priority areas is the chief challenge." Roper concentrated on making the mission real by setting three top priorities—children's health, prevention, and infrastructure.

"Every time I met with a group of employees or outsiders," says Roper, "I talked about these three areas. I used this discipline on myself and began every day by reminding myself that they were not only the organization's priorities but my personal priorities as well." Roper says that he knew he was successful when people began repeating the three priorities back to him. "It was then," he says, "that I truly felt that we were not 6,000 people heading off in different directions and that we were building on each other's efforts."

Managing through Mission

Here are former CDC director William Roper's tips for managing effectively for the mission:

- Choose your priorities.
- Avoid distraction.
- Push priorities; budget and plan around them.
- Don't let your in-box or telephone list decide what you're going to do; decide yourself.
- Monitor execution to judge success.

Stay Focused and Stick to the Mission

Once an organization has defined its mission and has set its priorities, it must address the challenge of sticking to that mission. This is particularly true in the nonprofit arena, where many practitioners such as The Nature Conservancy's vice president Greg Low have pegged the inability to stick to the mission as the greatest of all managerial failures. Many of those who work in nonprofits are deeply concerned about a number of social issues. In their commendable desire to do good, they have a tendency to try to push the organization into areas that, while often not far removed from the group's mission, can drain energy and resources from the pursuit of the main goals of the organization. At best, this leads to distraction. At worst, it can lead to the downfall of the organization itself.

The Nature Conservancy (TNC) is one of the wealthiest and most successful of nonprofits. It has the resources and talent to undertake almost any environmental project it desires. There is constant temptation, for example, to establish recreational areas or to join other nonprofits in lawsuits or lobbying efforts. TNC's leadership, however, has always understood that any deviation will dilute the organization's ability to accomplish its mission of saving endangered plant and animal species by acquiring and preserving the lands where they live.

"From the beginning," says TNC's Greg Low, "this organization made sure that its mission statement was brief, clear, and exactly to the point. It is a statement that was created with the consensus of everyone in the organization, one that through everything we publish and everything we communicate internally and externally is repeated over and over again. We have 130 business offices throughout the United States, in Latin America, and in various Pacific islands. If you ask any of our staff, volunteers, or trustees in any of these locales to state our mission, each person will say the same thing."

The Nature Conservancy is divided into nine regions. Each regional director operates with the understanding that, although making all workers aware of the mission is essential, inculcating in them a devotion to that mission is just as vital. "Our success," says Ron Geatz, TNC's director of member and partner communications, "is largely due to our narrow focus. We have a real fixation; we don't try to be all things to all people. We look around us and see all kinds of things we could get involved in—acid rain, affordable housing, animal rights—but we just don't think we can accomplish our specific mission if we dabble. We don't dabble."

TNC holds regular training sessions in which sticking to the mission is a primary topic. But it is in the way that the organization carries out its day-to-day work that its focus on mission is best fortified. "Any mission statement, no matter how brief, is broad by its very nature," says Greg Low. "More important, a mission statement doesn't tell you how to accomplish that mission. You will always have disputes among staff, employees, volunteers, and trustees as to what new projects should be initiated. It is through our countless strategy sessions that sticking to the mission becomes a reality. We treat any proposal for a new project seriously by considering not only its value, but by considering also what strategies would be needed to make the project work. If, during these deliberations, it becomes clear that the strategies or the project itself will divert energy from our stated mission, we reject that idea."

Putting the Mission Out Front

When Charles Bowsher was controller general of the General Accounting Office, one of his priorities was to make certain that everyone in the organization remained constantly aware of and focused on the agency's mission. The mission statement was printed on the memo pads and telephone answering pads used in every office. Each conference table and desk in these offices had a tent card perched upon it that also boldly proclaimed the mission statement.

If You Really Have to Change Your Mission

There are times when a mission must be changed. It is a high-risk strategy with a substantial payoff—if it is successful. The Nature Conservancy thrives by adhering to its narrow focus; by contrast, New York's Department of Juvenile Justice (DJJ) has made itself a model for counterparts throughout the nation by dramatically expanding its mission without diluting the agency's efficiency.

"We'd had twenty-seven directors in twenty-five years. The place was a pigpen and you could cut the tension with a knife." That, according to a veteran DJJ staffer, was Spofford (DJJ's secure juvenile detention facility) some fifteen years ago. More than 5,000 ten- to fifteen-year-olds are admitted to the facility each year, about 200 at any one time. The detainees have been charged with crimes ranging from grand theft to murder and are held while awaiting trial and during the trial process. Some are there for only a few days; others remain for up to a year.

It wasn't just Spofford that was in trouble. In the early 1980s, the department itself was in rough shape, a battered agency in the midst of political upheaval. Five years later the DJJ was regarded as one of the most innovative and effective agencies of its kind in the nation. Barry Krisberg, former president of the National Council on Crime and Delinquency, calls the improvement in the detention facility "the Spofford miracle." This remarkable turnaround began in 1983, when Ellen Schall became New York City's commissioner of juvenile justice. Schall approached her new position as head of the DJJ determined to change both the way the agency managed itself and the services it provided.

One of Schall's early moves was to hire Rose Washington as director of the Spofford facility. Washington, who in 1991 would succeed Schall as commissioner, started out by letting her staff know that she intended to do more than maintain the status quo.

"When our youngsters walk into Spofford," she told them, "and those doors lock behind them, they're in our hands, and we have a responsibility not only to make sure that they're safe but to make sure also that they are getting quality services. Never mind that this is a detention facility."

With Washington in place and with Assistant Commissioner Kathleen Feely as her right hand, Schall and her team began to develop her vision for the organization. She realized they had to convince staff to buy into a whole new way of doing business. "Revitalization," said Schall, "goes beyond specific program initiatives and is about change in the very fabric of the organization. One must invest in the organization in order to revitalize it. This involves finding the organization's strengths and building on them. This entails a primary focus on the foundations of the organization: its people, culture, structure, reward systems, patterns of communication, values, and mission. It's long-term, slow, patient work."

Schall and her executive staff began to communicate their vision of detention as "a window of opportunity, a chance to make a difference in a child's life." They were determined to extend the DJJ's stated mission to include care as well as custody.

"We knew," says Schall, "that expanding the mission would be risky business. After all, people come to this work because they care about the organization's mission." Mindful of honoring the mission as a contract between an organization and its employees, Schall and her top staff made sure that they did not mandate the change from above. They began to negotiate it from within. "Building an agenda and developing a mission," says Schall, "has to be done in constant conversation with your staff. It doesn't work and it won't outlast you if it's something that's just yours."

"Specifically," says Kathleen Feely, "we put together a team of representatives from every part of the agency and went on a retreat. We wrote a mission statement that made care as important as custody. We realized that we were dealing with kids who had failed at everything they had tried—even crime—so a key phrase we began to use was, 'giving kids the opportunity to have a successful experience.'"

The next step was to redesign programs and develop new services to put the new mission statement into action, including:

Health care. The majority of children detained at Spofford had not seen a doctor in years. Now, within five days of admission, each child's dental, physical, and mental health is assessed. Necessary treatment is provided on site. Spofford's mental health unit is available to follow up on referrals, to provide ongoing counseling, and to advise staff.

Schooling. Although the average age of children at Spofford is fifteen, 34 percent read below the fourth-grade level at the time of admission. The Spofford staff established a five-day-a-week educational program, with small classes grouped by reading levels. "It doesn't matter if a youngster is here for two weeks or six months," says Spofford's former deputy director for education Roy Davenport. "Our job is to show him that he can learn, that he can succeed, and that there are people who really care about his success."

Nonsecure detention. Through a citywide network of group and foster homes, the DJJ developed a nonsecure detention program for juveniles who do not need to be locked up. Approximately eighty youngsters reside in these facilities. They attend school daily and participate in recreation, group counseling, and tutoring programs.

Aftercare. Aftercare is a program that follows about 1,000 youngsters as they return to home and school. Aftercare case managers work with families and children and community agencies to coordinate services. Says one case worker, "Getting a kid out of detention is not the whole issue. The issue is getting him back to school, putting him back into the mainstream, and helping him make that adjustment." An independent audit of the program has shown that aftercare reduces recidivism, or repeat offenses. Those few youths in the program who were rearrested were arrested less frequently and for less serious crimes.

Family support. For those children who don't need detention but aren't supervised adequately at home, the DJJ's counselors work with children and their families to identify problem areas, set target goals, and develop new skills to reach these goals.

The DJJ's ability "to get the job done" through the expansion of its mission has resulted in significant benefits both for the young people it serves and for New York's taxpayers. The agency's programs have helped scores of troubled youngsters begin crime-free, productive lives. Thanks in great measure to its inspired expansion of mission, the DJJ is today regarded by many in the juvenile justice field as the most innovative and effective agency of its kind in the nation. "What DJJ has achieved," says Barry Krisberg, "sends a clear message that juvenile detention centers can provide safe and humane care to troubled youngsters. Spofford should remind us that abuse and second-rate care of delinquent youth are unacceptable and not inevitable."

Tips for Expanding the Mission

Rose Washington, former commissioner of New York's Department of Juvenile Justice, provides the following guidelines for a successful expansion of mission:

- Deliberate long and hard before undertaking any expansion of mission. Involve staff and employees from every level of the organization in these deliberations.
- Consider whether expansion will, in any way, impede carrying out your present mission as stated.
- Make a list of all the benefits you believe will be derived from an expansion of mission. Get input from all levels of the organization.
- In concert with staff and employees, set goals and objectives for concrete programs that will make the expansion an effective reality.
- Start small. Use pilot programs to iron out the kinks and build small successes. Build on these successes.
- Celebrate each small win on the road to expansion.

Flying High

When Rose Washington took over as director of Spofford, she began her first address to her staff with a story: "An airplane," she told them, "had just taken off when the copilot noticed that a rat was gnawing on the fuel line. In a panic, he informed the pilot of what was happening, but the pilot continued the plane's ascension. More panicked than ever, the copilot screamed out his warning again. The pilot kept accelerating and then turned to the copilot saying, 'Don't worry. We're going to fly so high that no rat will live.' That," Washington told her troops, "is what this facility is going to do."

The next day "Higher than Rats" buttons began showing up on the sweaters and jackets of the staff. The phrase became an important slogan throughout the agency.

Use the Mission as a Recruiting Tool

Few government agencies or nonprofits can offer salaries that compete with their corporate counterparts. But when it comes to recruiting, the mission can bridge the salary gap. With high purpose, some public-service organizations can attract the best talent to perform at high levels under less-than-ideal conditions. Many agencies—

the Peace Corps, Head Start, and Doctors without Borders, for example—attract highly talented people without participating in a bidding war.

Because of its mission, the General Accounting Office (GAO) has attracted some of the best young lawyers, accountants, economists, and other experts to the agency. Recruiting standards at the GAO are extremely high. In order to be considered, candidates must have an overall grade point average of 3.0 on a 4-point scale and must be in the top third of their graduating class. Like other government agencies, the GAO has, on occasion, been caught in a full or partial firing freeze, but in a typical year, the agency receives more than 7,000 applications for 200 available professional jobs.

"The nature of our mission is the best selling tool we have," says Steve Kenealy, deputy director of the GAO's Office of Recruitment. "Most of our recruits come from graduate schools of public administration and are familiar with the mission and the work of the GAO. Typically they are young people who have a strong desire to help government perform better. They are aware that the work that this agency carries out is both exciting and important. I'm also struck by the fact that a great many of our new hires tell us that they chose the GAO because our standards are so high and because assignments within the agency continually change. Money will always be an important factor, but what we have found is that for so many young people today, obtaining a job that will constantly challenge them is the key issue. Our mission certainly supplies them with that opportunity."

Mission also enables the Centers for Disease Control and Prevention to attract some of the best and the brightest. Each July, some sixty physicians, along with a smaller number of public health workers, veterinarians, and statisticians chosen from an enormous list of applicants, enter the elite training program of the CDC's Epidemic Intelligence Service (EIS). Although the pay is not impressive, a position at EIS is regarded as equivalent in professional challenge and stature to a clerkship in the U.S. Supreme Court. Like Supreme Court clerks, EIS trainees proceed on a fast track to leadership in their field. After a month's training, EIS officers are deployed, one-third to the field, two-thirds to national headquarters in Atlanta as front-line workers in epidemics and other public-health threats. Some trainees study radiation leaks, some bathtub injuries. Others are sent to work with local health authorities, and some are sent abroad.

This training brings significant results. The first telephone call that Dr. Jim Beecham received as a new EIS officer in brought a report of an unknown respiratory illness among conventioneers in Philadelphia in the summer of 1976. Beecham's team spent six months tracking down the bacterial culprit (later named Legionnaire's Disease). Another EIS officer, Dr. Wayne Shandera, who was posted to Los Angeles, traced an increase in occurrences of a rare type of pneumonia, *pneumonocystis carnii*, and found five cases, all in men under forty who were active homosexuals. His findings were published in the CDC's *Morbidity and Mortality Weekly Report*—the first report of the disease now known as Acquired Immune Deficiency Syndrome, or AIDS.

In the nonprofit sector, the San Diego Zoo's passion for conservation has enabled it to attract highly qualified men and women in a highly competitive job market. Zoo officials proudly relate the story of the woman applicant with an M.B.A. who was so committed to the mission of the zoo that she took a job as an assistant camel keeper while waiting for a job opening related to her professional training. A compelling mission backed by solid execution attracts the best job candidates and motivates employees to perform at their peak. (There's an old story of two stone masons, one skilled and dedicated, the other a time server. The difference between the two? Mission. When each was asked what he did for a living, the time server said he cut stone. The performer replied, "I'm building a cathedral.")

The words have changed slightly over the years, but the zoo's basic mission of conservation and wonder has remained the same and is part of the experience of every employee and visitor. After each animal show, trainers talk to the audience about how to help save wildlife. And the animals themselves are used as vehicles for imparting the mission. Animal training supervisor Kathy Marmack calls her animals "ambassadors for the message of conservation and preservation." This dedication to mission extends even to those employees who don't work directly with the zoo's creatures and plants. Says one gift shop employee, "We don't do Earth Day once a year. We do it all the time." Every item in the gift shop is chosen to carry a message of wildlife and habitat awareness. Each item has a story, and each employee is trained to tell that story. And each story focuses on the society's mission.

Mission as the Unifying Force

Sandra Stiner Lowe, the driving force behind Fairfax County's Medical Care for Children Project, credits much of the project's success to the manner in which everyone involved is driven by its mission. Here is Sandy Lowe's formula for maintaining mission as a unifying force:

- Put the mission statement out there for everyone to see. Make certain that "everyone" includes customers as well as staff, both employees and volunteers.   ◆▸

> **Mission as the Unifying Force** (continued)
>
> - Make sure that everyone at every level understands that those at the top are committed to the mission and that the mission reflects their vision for the organization.
> - Create mechanisms (feedback sessions, training courses, retreats) to make certain that everyone fully understands the mission. Ask everyone on a regular basis what he or she is doing to keep the mission alive and active.
> - Make revisiting the mission a part of your yearly agenda. Involve everyone in ascertaining whether the mission statement accurately reflects the purpose, goals, and objectives of the organization.
> - Demonstrate a total commitment to sticking to the mission. Avoid temptations to stray off course, no matter how attractive these temptations might be.

Defining the organization's mission, knowing when to stick tenaciously to it, and determining when to make necessary changes represent the beginnings of an organization's march to effectiveness. But every organization and all those who work within it must realize that it takes much more to succeed. Even the most mission-oriented organizations will run into rough waters if they don't understand that in today's world change is a constant and that coping with change is one of the greatest managerial challenges. In the next chapter we will see how those organizations that flourish not only accept change but embrace it as a positive force.

2

THE CHALLENGE
OF CHANGE

If you always do what you always did, you'll always get what you always got." That's how one public-sector manager we interviewed characterized the constant need for change. One thing that managers in all sectors are in agreement about is that in today's world change is not only necessary for top performance, it is often the key to survival.

Those who work in the government sector are no strangers to change. As another public-sector manager reminded us, "Under our political system, we face the prospect of a hostile takeover every four years." The Clinton administration attempted to streamline federal agencies through its reinventing government program. Some government managers have championed the reengineering approach, advocating total change in their most basic work processes.

Nonprofits are also undergoing radical changes. Shrinking federal funds, increasing competition for private funds, and a changing volunteer pool have profoundly altered the way many of these organizations must operate. And this has happened at a time when, because of downsized federal agencies, they are being asked to do even more with less.

Change in our era is fast, extreme, and often unpredictable. Every public agency and nonprofit organization is faced with the challenge of how to respond. The vanguard organizations we studied understand that merely adapting to change is not enough. They must commit to change. They embrace change as a way of life. They are alert to what's happening in the world, and they are constantly rethinking their place in it. All operate with the understanding that in order to continually revitalize an organization, you must:

- Make change your ally to revitalize your organization.
- Combat resistance by supporting change from the top.
- Use budget as an agent of change.
- Realize that big changes require broad initiatives—and bold risks.
- Tolerate mistakes and learn from them.
- Keep changing even when you're on top.
- Understand that change begins with customers.
- Give your change champions the power to implement new ideas.
- Listen to champions who challenge you.
- Dare to act quickly.
- Understand that the foundation of change is small starts.
- Practice creative swiping.

Make Change Your Ally to Revitalize Your Organization

The best example we encountered of an organization that has faced up to the challenge of change is the nonprofit giant Girl Scouts of the U.S.A. (GSUSA). The Girl Scouts provides a model for how an organization can embrace change while holding on to traditional strengths and longtime organizational values.

Unlike General Motors, IBM, or Avon, the Girl Scouts came through the massive changes of the 1980s and entered the 1990s without stumbling. In fact, as the nineties began, the Girl Scouts were bigger, stronger, and savvier than they had been a decade before. That is a considerable achievement when one considers that in 1976, when Frances Hesselbein took over as national executive director, the organization's future seemed anything but bright. In terms of prestige and public stature, the sixties and seventies had not been kind. Women's roles had changed radically, and much of the public felt that the Girl Scouts were lagging behind that change. The image of white girls in knee socks tying knots and learning campfire songs in suburban basements seemed out of touch with the times. And nothing reflected these attitudes more dramatically than the 33 percent drop in the organization's membership.

On the positive side, Girl Scouting had a national base and a strong and proud tradition. There were hundreds of thousands of adult volunteers and millions more "graduates," each with a stake in perpetuating the image and ideals of the Girl Scouts. But could an organization so deeply committed to tradition embrace profound changes in values, lifestyles, and demography? What kind of programs would reach today's girls? Would management be able to effectively guide an organization of three million members dispersed through 333 separate corporations and 190,000 troops? How would the Girl Scouts of yesterday, many of whom had become the volunteers of today, react as the organization changed?

As a first step, Hesselbein and the national staff, working with a dedicated and capable national board, launched a major reexamination of the organization's mission in today's world. As laid down in its constitution, that mission entails "inspiring girls with the highest ideals of character, conduct, patriotism, and service that they may become happy and resourceful citizens." But what did those words mean in the late 1970s? The national board, along with representatives of all 333 councils, gathered together to tackle the task of redefining the organization while remaining true to its mission. Specifically, they sought answers to three basic questions:

1. *What is our business?* After much deliberation, the group came to the conclusion that the GSUSA was in business "to help girls grow and reach their highest potential." This ideal is now deeply imbued in today's Girl Scout culture, and we often heard the phrase used as a yardstick to measure every program and enterprise.
2. *Who are our customers?* What are girls, aged five to seventeen, like today? Who is drawn to Girl Scouting? What do they get from the experience? Who is left out? Why? The carefully researched answers to these questions became the foundation of a new commitment to diversity.
3. *What's good for the girls?* Information on customers, gathered from surveys and a biennial "Environmental Scanning Report," circulated throughout the organization. Today, "Is it good for the girls?" has become a challenge that everyone in the organization is expected to address.

Next, the staff and volunteers began to develop a nationwide corporate planning and management system to professionalize their operations and those of the 333 councils. They developed guidelines on communications, corporate planning, council self-evaluations, effective boards of directors, fund development, and financial reporting and published them as a series of monographs. Today these books are not only used by the Girl Scouts and their councils, but they also have been adopted by other organizations, such as the Port Authority of New York and New Jersey, United Way of America, the University of Virginia Graduate School of Business, and Volunteers of America.

The Girl Scouts' management then began to make changes to reverse the decline in membership. Market studies told them their customer group was changing. The organization and its programs had to focus on reaching out to girls from all social and ethnic backgrounds. An important step in making membership more accessible to these groups was establishing the Daisy Scouts for five-year-olds. The national board and GSUSA's staff saw in Daisy Scouting the opportunity to serve "latchkey" girls and other youngsters who, thanks to their exposure to television, were often sophisticated beyond their years. Today, there are some 190,000 Daisy Girl Scouts in America, and they represent the fastest-growing segment of Girl Scouting. Says management sage Peter Drucker, "Daisy Girl Scouts is so far the only program that has seen these critical demographic changes and children's exposure to long hours of TV viewing as an opportunity."

GSUSA has met the challenge of change with great success. More important, it has developed surveys, strategies, and structures that will allow it to keep pace with change. The organization is open to change everywhere—at every level and location.

Take, for example, the Girl Scouts' commitment to diversity. That commitment is reinforced everywhere. At the top, it is exemplified by current national executive director Mary Rose Main, who says, "We *have* to be diverse. We have to be at the leading edge in helping girls with the tough issues they face on the street, in the schools, in the community." The national staff makes sure that the meaning of the mission is spread to every corner of the organization by communicating ceaselessly, relating diversity to mission and mission to the humblest task or program. As a result, the commitment to diversity permeates every system and structure, incorporating it in goal setting, personnel evaluation, recruiting and hiring, communications, and training.

The national board sets this commitment to diversity, but *how* Girl Scouting becomes more diverse is up to individual councils. Line managers are expected to use the information, training, and support provided by national headquarters to translate policy into specific programs that will reach new girls. The strategy of placing authority in the hands of the line managers has unleashed innovation at the local level. For example:

- The Northwest Georgia Council in Atlanta has established fifteen troops composed of girls who live in homeless shelters. Troops serving economically deprived girls have also been set up in low-income housing projects. In addition, troops have been established for Hispanic mothers and daughters, while troops for Vietnamese youngsters are in the planning stage. The council also operates a Girl Scout troop in the Fulton County Juvenile Probation System, which serves first-time probationers.
- The Kennebec, Maine, Girl Scout Council runs a drop-in center, A Place for Girls, which sponsors after-school and summer activities for girls from low-income families. Lo-

cated in South Portland, Maine, the center attracts many recent refugees, primarily from Asia and eastern Europe. A Place for Girls has become so important to the nine- to twelve-year-olds for which it was established that the program was expanded to allow the girls to continue after their twelfth birthday. And they have opened the program to eight-year-olds as well. In 1996, in collaboration with Portland's Mad Horse Theatre and the East End Children's Workshop, the Girl Scouts founded a theatrical production project. Part of the Place for Girls program, its purpose is to involve youngsters in every phase of the theatrical experience as a way of helping them learn how to work and accomplish together.

- Since some girls can't fit in scouting activities after school, the GSUSA established "Girl Scouting in the School Day," The Tejas Girl Scout Council in Dallas, Texas, has expanded their program to communities throughout the eastern part of the state. Designed for girls in the sixth, seventh, and eighth grades, the program's activities focus on such issues as diversity, self-esteem, leadership, and physical fitness. The behavior of girls enrolled in the program has improved so dramatically that the Tejas council now faces the challenge of accommodating an ever-increasing number of requests from schools that wish to participate.

When an organization sets a new course, it always encounters some resistance to change. People tend to divide into two camps, traditionalists and innovators. The GSUSA was no exception, but as the organization changed course to become more diverse and to bring contemporary issues and problems into the program, management found a unique way to link innovation and tradition and, in the process, take some of the sting out of resistance. By reshaping the past, they made a new future easier to swallow. For example, Juliette Low, founder of the Girl Scouts, was an eccentric who had boldly taken girls camping before their mothers had won the right to vote. In the 1980s, the Girl Scouts, through their literature, began portraying the way she appeared to her contemporaries—as an independent woman of action, a real risk taker. And to make the goal of diversity more palatable to conservative members of the Scouting family, management began to document the Girl Scouts' long tradition of diversity. For instance, they publicized the fact that as early as 1917 the organization had welcomed physically disabled girls into its ranks, and that as far back as 1930 Native American girls had been proud Girl Scouts.

By any measure, the focus on embracing new realities has dramatically revitalized the Girl Scouts. Membership decline has been reversed, and the fastest-growing segment of this membership is represented by girls from racial and ethnic minorities.

A Changing Work Force

During his tenure from 1981 to 1996, Comptroller General Charles Bowsher, director of the General Accounting Office (GAO), focused particular attention on what he sees as the main issue of the nineties and beyond. "Any organization operating in the past twenty years," he says, "has had to handle the issue of diversity of its employee work force. If, as an organization, you haven't handled this successfully, you're going to be behind the power curve in the next ten to twenty years. I spent a lot of effort making sure that GAO will be representative of this country in minorities and women. A lot of organizations have not understood that we're going to have a different mix of work force in the future. If you haven't figured that out and done something about it, you're not going to have a strong organization in the years ahead."

Combat Resistance by Supporting Change from the Top

Another remarkable turnaround we encountered during our investigations was that made by the U.S. Forest Service. Thanks to an innovative pilot program initiated in several forests throughout the nation, the Forest Service became a dramatic example of the way positive change can be achieved in government. Of all the forests involved in the pilot project, the Ochoco Forest in Prineville, Oregon, was fastest out of the gate and achieved the widest range of effective change. The key to Ochoco's success was the way in which management supported workers in making the difficult transition to new ways of doing business.

"As a government agency, the Forest Service has always been pretty rule-bound," says Ochoco's team leader for financial resources, J. C. Hansen. "Before the pilot program, people were used to having iron-clad regulations there to protect them. When we replaced the rule books that took up seventeen feet of shelf space with a simple forty-one-page manual, a lot of our staff and employees really freaked."

According to Hansen, this anxiety was overcome in two specific ways. First, management made it clear that new ways of doing things on employees' own initiative would be fully supported by top management. "People," says Hansen, "needed time to adjust to their new freedom. I used to tell them, 'Don't worry, when they come for you tell them I told you to do it. I'll go to jail.'"

Second, Hansen and his fellow Ochoco managers operated with the understanding that old habits die hard and that one of their top priorities had to be that of continually encouraging employees to use their new decision-making authority by trying out any new ideas or methods they felt would improve things. "What it all boils down to," says Hansen, "is that when you open up the cage, not all the animals come out. Sometimes, you have to beat them out."

Perhaps the most important lesson of the Ochoco experience is the way it provides concrete evidence of the effectiveness of pilot programs. The pilot enabled managers and employees to get accustomed to new ideas, to correct inevitable mistakes, and to build upon the lessons and successes of the pilot when expanding the program or approach.

And, as we discovered, it is these lessons and successes that outlast the pilot itself. The pilot program at Ochoco has come to an end; however, the lessons remain valid. "Now," says administrative officer Rod Collins, "when our people run into a barrier, they don't give up; they remember the pilot. Specifically, they don't say, 'Where does it state I can do that?' Now they say, 'Where in the manual does it say I *can't* do that?'"

Benefits of a Pilot Program

Administrative officer Rod Collins was deeply involved in the U.S. Forest Service's pilot program. Here is a short list of what he sees as the greatest benefits of pilots in general:

- Pilot programs help make leaders visible.
- Pilots make for small units. In small units, people talk with each other.
- During a pilot experience, all change is blamed on the pilot. During a pilot experience, all change is credited to the pilot. Both points of view are correct.
- To be effective, a pilot must allow for employee freedom and provide employee incentives. This leads to a spirited organization. With spirit, everything is possible. Without it, nothing seems to work right.

Bringing about Change in Government Agencies

Included in what the U.S. Forest Service terms its "lessons of the pilot" are the following rules of thumb for bringing about change in government agencies:

- Restructuring requires strong leadership and must be initiated from the top down. People will not be willing to undergo a cultural change without assurance and inspiration from top management.
- It is not enough just to streamline programs or eliminate regulations. Work conditions, signals, behavioral norms, and expectations also need to be changed.   ◆▶

Bringing about Change in Government Agencies (continued)

- A government agency's competitive edge in the future will be tied to nonconformity, diversity, and individual talent. In recruiting and hiring employees, our managers should ask, "How will this person contribute to overcoming the bureaucracy and to our competitiveness?" rather than "Does he or she fit into our organization?"
- In holding managers at all levels accountable, the emphasis needs to be shifted from keeping the boss out of trouble to a focus on end results. Rewards and incentives should be based on the bottom line.
- Management can empower government workers to make full use of their talents, innovations, and ideas by removing barriers to initiative and creativity. One of the first steps is to allow employees to take a larger role in management by helping to design their organizations, participating in productivity improvements, rating their progress and accomplishments, and even selecting superiors.
- Government agencies—and all organizations—must operate on the principle that change is not a win-lose proposition but an opportunity to express individuality and creativity that will aid the organization in accomplishing its mission most effectively.

Use Budget as an Agent of Change

In most organizations, accounting is the most powerfully conservative force. We have all seen the most promising programs trip and fall on accounting procedures. The pilot program in the Ochoco Forest demonstrated to us how finance molds behavior. Its power can be used either to preserve the status quo or to fuel profound organizational change.

By changing over to lump-sum budgeting and allowing pilot forests to keep any savings, the Forest Service created a climate for change. In the four pilot units, the standard fifty-five budget items were reduced to a few major appropriation categories, and Washington sent the pilot locations their budget allocations in three or four lump sums. This was a 180-degree turnaround from the way most government organizations and large corporations manage their budgets by fastidiously tracking tiny little bits of money.

Micromanaging budgets is a serious problem. Experts report that when you add tracking and reporting, 10 to 20 percent of a government agency's total resources may be spent on the administrative function of budgeting. The Ochoco Forest took lump-sum budgeting to its logical extreme and put together one bucket of money.

All the money went toward the operation of the forest, and the people in the forest decided how it was to be spent for the best results. Redefining the way the money came down from Washington in effect redefined the way work was carried out. Teams began working together to get the job done, rather than looking at the budget for direction in how to do their jobs. Says J. C. Hansen, "When the money came down in the little boxes, it put the employees in the boxes. They had twenty-seven different slices to protect and maintain. And the implication was that our resources people do not know what they're doing, didn't know what jobs to do, couldn't identify their priorities. They said, 'You're a forester, you're a range person, you're a wildlife person. Work until that box is empty and then we'll find something else for you to do.' They had little consideration at all for the total job that needed to be done or for the fact that one box might be able to do the job and save money, but you could never hand it to the guy in the next box who was starving. So when the Chief gave us the authority to get the money in one bucket and allowed us to operate as we saw fit from that one bucket, it changed everything. We could make the rules. And that was an enormous breakthrough for our people."

As one official comments, "Employees learned how to talk with one another again. As we stripped back the protection of the bureaucracy, we found trust, a term not commonly used in budget language, to be more and more important. And with it grew a sense of total organization, not a fragmented one aligned with budget line items."

J. C. Hansen points out that the experience was not without its problems. In the first year, Ochoco overspent by $250,000. The next year, that amount was held back from the budget and employees made up the shortfall. But, insists Hansen, accountability did not suffer by lumping all the money together. "Our people took all that money and ran—right back to the forest where it was spent on improvements."

Big Changes Require Broad Initiatives and Bold Risks

In 1985, the Urban League of Rochester decided to mark its twentieth anniversary by focusing on the state of the city's educational system. It appointed a task force of community representatives to study the situation and to make specific recommendations for improvement. In March 1986, the task force published its findings under the title *A Call to Action*. The report began: "There is a crisis in our community. We are failing our young people, failing to adequately prepare them to assume their roles, failing to prepare them to cope in the society we have created." The committee documented the alarming figures on absenteeism and dropout rates as well as low academic achievement that characterized the Rochester city schools. *A Call to Action* then set forth detailed recommendations for action.

At the same time that the Urban League's report was being prepared, the acting superintendent of schools, Peter McWalters, was writing an eighteen-page mission statement for the school district. McWalters's document was, in fact, far more than a mission statement. It was a detailed blueprint for the total reform of the Rochester schools.

Among its many recommendations, McWalters's document spelled out a strict new set of standards for all of Rochester's teachers, outlined a reward plan for those teachers who exceeded the standards, and called for the creation of a system of peer performance review. McWalters's report detailed ways in which every facet of the Rochester community at large would be recruited to play an active role in total school reform. The blueprint also recommended the implementation of a training program for principals and called for the establishment of a program through which experienced teachers would serve as mentors, sharing their talents and experience with first- and second-year teachers to help them develop the skills needed to succeed in an urban school setting. The document placed special emphasis on the need to establish a citywide school-based management program.

Tolerate Mistakes and Learn from Them

For more than a decade, Rochester's school reformers have been attempting to successfully implement all of these reforms. They have achieved substantial success in varied areas. Several of the pilot programs they initiated in the elementary schools have been effective. The school-based management program has led to significant positive changes. Particularly successful has been the establishment of school/business partnerships. However, in taking on a challenge that would break the backs of many, Rochester's reformers freely admit that the overall results have been mixed and that many mistakes have been made. But they are also strong in their conviction that they have learned important lessons from their errors, lessons that can teach all organizations much about what is needed to bring about significant change.

As we talked to school officials, teachers, parents, and members of the Rochester business community, it was apparent that one of the basic mistakes made early on in the change effort was that of raising unrealistic expectations about how long it would take for widespread reform to take hold. "We have to stop promising people astronomical results in the short term," says assistant district superintendent Loretta Johnson. "We're trying to move this district into the twenty-first century, both instructionally and professionally. Everyone has to understand that fundamental change takes real time."

When the reform movement began, Superintendent McWalters and Adam Urbanski, head of the Rochester Teachers' Union, assumed the task of chief spokesmen for the effort. They accomplished much, but many of those most committed to the reform now believe that it was a mistake to have depended so heavily on McWalters and Urbanski to "sell" the new programs and approach. "Peter and Adam are super salesmen," says former district legal counsel Adam Kaufman. "But by their taking on so much of this responsibility, other important people in the community were left out. If you want to involve the entire community, you've got to give leaders from every segment of that community a vested interest in making change happen."

Another shortcoming pointed out to us by several school officials had to do with not getting the news out when real progress was made. "One of our real failures," says former school board president Catherine Spoto, "was that we weren't able to convey our incremental progress to the community. We made enormous strides in our elementary program. And that will carry right through to the senior highs when the youngsters get there. But we haven't done a good job in getting this across to the community." Says Peter McWalters, "We haven't understood the need to put in place something that's the equivalent of a public affairs department, something that can engage the community. Interestingly enough, we have been good at getting the news out about progress one school at a time, but we don't do it effectively as a central exercise."

McWalters is the first to admit what he and others perceive as the most serious mistake of all. "When we began our reform," he says, "the decision was made to hit the institution with as many shocks at one time as we could in order to loosen it up. We decided to do everything. In a three-year period we reorganized the secondary schools, put in middle schools, established school-based management, set up Home Base Guidance, began to set performance and accountability standards for teachers, and created peer intervention through our Mentor Program. We knew we were disturbing the equilibrium, but we felt that we had eighteen months before the culture would start to atrophy again. Our biggest mistake was that from the beginning, we never put into place the necessary mechanisms to manage change once it began to happen."

Rochester's Blueprint for Change

We asked a group of those involved in the reform effort to summarize for us what they now regard as the essentials for bringing about meaningful change:

- Understand that real change takes time to achieve.
- Don't promise more than you can realistically deliver.
- Give as many people as you can, both inside and outside the organization, a true, vested interest in making change happen.
- Celebrate every achievement, no matter how small. Get the good news out in as many forums as you can.
- Establish a planning procedure for every step of the change process. Involve people from every level of the organization in each planning procedure.
- Wherever possible, begin each new venture with a pilot program. Get the kinks out before expanding the program.
- Create a training program for each new program you initiate.
- Admit your mistakes. Learn from them. Move forward.

Keep Changing Even When You're on Top

Most organizations commit to change only when they are in trouble. But the most successful organizations understand that they must explore change even during the good times. The Children's Museum of Indianapolis, established more than seventy years ago, is the largest and arguably most effective children's museum in the world. Its staff, both employees and unpaid workers, are outstanding and they know it. Still, they are not satisfied. They are constantly questioning themselves, seeking new approaches, and pushing for change and improvement. This restlessness and ambition are shared by everyone, but it is more than an attitude; it is an organizationwide strategy. Says museum president Peter Sterling, "You're most vulnerable when you are at the top of your game because other people copy you and cut into your market. When you are at the top, that is when you have to be most innovative to stay there. Larry Bird didn't stop practicing and taking foul shots every day because he was great. At the same time as he got older he changed his game." Former board chairperson Pat Turner-Smith speaks for her colleagues when she states, "We must get people who, especially in the Midwest, were brought up on the theory that 'if it's not broke, don't fix it' to understand and buy into the need to change to achieve continued and greater levels of excellence."

The Children's Museum of Indianapolis attracts more than a million visitors each year. The museum houses more than 110,000 artifacts, 10,000 of which are on display at any one time. In addition, the museum creates and puts into the hands of children several thousand programs every year. "We have been a great museum *for* kids," says Peter Sterling, "but our objective now is to be a great museum *with* kids, and that's an entirely different mission."

Being a museum with as well as for children entails developing programs, exhibitions, and activities that allow youngsters to participate actively in the learning process. It also means getting young people involved, wherever possible, in creating these projects.

The sheer volume of the museum's programs and exhibits reflects a restlessness and a commitment to change and improvement that is a way of life at the museum. "This," says Paul Richard, executive vice president, "is a place where no one is ever satisfied. We go out and visit other places, realize how much better we are doing things, and then sit down and figure out how to do better." As one staff member describes it, "I never planned to work in one place for very long, but this museum changes so much that I have really worked for three different museums in my six years here."

To maintain a constant pattern of change, the museum places great emphasis on research and development. Staff members seek out the world's experts in history, geography, science, art, and archaeology and ask them to assess the museum's existing activities and to help plan new ones. Some of the best minds in the world are delighted to serve the inquisitive minds of children. "We try to find people," says Paul Richard, "who are at the forefront of specific areas and bring them out here to work with our staff. That is part of our R&D. And it's this research and development that is one of the things that differentiates us from other institutions who are spending very little on R&D, particularly in education. We do R&D of all types, for every program, whether we're sitting down with the kids or dealing with futurists at the Hudson Institute."

"I don't know what happened to General Motors," says Peter Sterling, "or some of the others who were on top, but there is a tendency to stay home and admire how well you do things. But when you get big and good you have to be careful to look at what's going on. We constantly strive to lower our walls and raise our antennae."

Keeping Change Constant

"Although we are big and good," says Peter Sterling, "we are still innovators. We show that while we are an elephant, we can still dance. We're more than seventy years young and still growing." In order to keep change constant, the museum continually circulates lists of questions to all employees and acts upon the feedback it receives. An example: ➡

Keeping Change Constant (continued)

1. How can we increase the effectiveness of soliciting information from our public about exhibition/program plans, collection directions, store merchandise, admissions, etc.?
2. How should the museum position itself in the Indianapolis community?
3. Nationally?
4. What improvements could be made to communicate important information to/from the staff?
5. Where should we "wander" when we are wandering around?
6. How should we use our collections more effectively?
7. What questions should we ask our visitors?
8. How can we make our training programs more effective?
9. What specific improvements do you suggest for our phone system?
10. Should we meet once a month (four hours), bi-weekly (two hours), weekly (one hour), or not at all?
11. How can we make the museum more emotionally/psychologically accessible?

It's easy to get caught up in the managing process. But getting the job done means going beyond process and focusing on outcomes. It means monitoring everyone's performance and continually assessing whether goals are being met. In the next chapter, we'll meet some results-oriented champions and discover how they deal with one of the most demanding of all management challenges.

3

THE CHALLENGE OF
MANAGING FOR RESULTS

One of the most common criticisms leveled at public agencies and nonprofits is that they are "process oriented," focusing on *how* things are done rather than *what* needs to get done, more committed to rules and regulations than to results. According to the critics, this process orientation is one of the main reasons that nonprofits and government agencies in particular tend to be slow, wasteful, and unproductive.

Like any half-truth, this criticism distorts and conceals as much as it reveals. It is true that government is "process oriented." That is precisely what we pay for it to be. We don't want government to deliver its goods and services as a private business would; rather, we ask it to function in such a way that the humblest citizen will have the same access to services as the richest and most powerful. Nonprofits share a process orientation though their circumstances are slightly different. Many of them have missions that demand they serve not only those who have the wherewithal to demand service, but all who are in need. As stewards of the public good, these organizations must be both equitable and efficient.

The problem of efficiency is complicated by the very nature of the tasks government and nonprofits undertake and how they are funded. The more crime there is, the more money goes to law enforcement. When crime drops—perhaps because the police are doing an effective job—funding is usually cut back. Where, then, are the incentives to improve public safety? As another example, most school districts are funded according to how many students attend school there. How many are compensated for the number of youngsters who get a quality education and leave school with the ability to continue their educations and hold down jobs?

The organizations profiled in this chapter are top performers by the numbers. They have pioneered programs that keep their organizational focus on results rather than process. They have struggled to monitor performance for their customers; many have adopted aggressive quality programs to that end. They lead the way in focusing on outcomes and results. They keep score by the numbers and assess progress qualitatively. They have a clear vision of what success will look like and how far they have come along the road toward that goal. They differentiate between high performers and nonperformers. They hold everyone accountable. They reward performance—sometimes with money, sometimes by celebrating accomplishments. Most important, the best public-service organizations have developed powerful strategies to focus on and improve outcomes while staying true to their mission of service. And they understand the following guidelines:

- Managing for results begins with careful planning.
- Everyone needs to be held accountable for performance.
- They must organize to act quickly.
- They can boost results by sharing power.
- Power sharing can be supercharged.
- Performance needs to be measured in customers' terms.
- They must use their boards to maximize their results.
- They need to use the books to keep score.

Managing for Results Begins with Careful Planning

To manage for results, you must first articulate the results you are after. The Government Accounting Office (GAO) is in the results business. As the government's accounting and evaluation firm, it audits and evaluates a staggering number of programs and activities and issues detailed reports on each of them. The GAO continually has to address such questions as "How much did it cost—and why? How will it affect jobs? Was the money spent in an effective manner?" The GAO has to come up with the answers to these questions while navigating partisan politics and bureaucratic turf wars, without jeopardizing its close relationship to its prime customer, the U.S. Congress, or losing its objectivity. In order to make progress under these difficult circumstances, GAO managers must plan, plan, plan.

"To be flexible, we break our work down into planning issue areas," says the GAO's former head, Comptroller General Charles Bowsher. "We have a long-term strategic plan in each of these areas and an annual plan in each of these areas as well. But if something happens in an area, then we have to quickly change the plan. Before Chernobyl, we were trying to reduce the amount of work and the accompanying planning we did in nuclear energy because it wasn't as important as it had been ten years earlier. However, with that incident everyone wanted to know how safe our nuclear plants were and our people in that area had to quickly readjust their planning strategies in order to renew their efforts."

Every issue area director is responsible for developing both long-range and short-term plans and is expected to be able to change these plans quickly according to current world developments. For instance, scandals at the Department of Housing and Urban Development, in the nation's banking system, and in defense procurement prompted the GAO to develop plans for targeting specific programs that are highly vulnerable to fraud. Fourteen high-risk areas were singled out for attention and multidisciplinary teams were formed to track events and report findings.

All of this activity, like almost all that the GAO does, was coordinated with the needs of various Congressional committees. "Our planning process," says Bowsher, "includes extensive meetings with Congressional staff, with staff from other agencies, and with outside interest groups."

KQS

Managing for results doesn't have to be complicated. Principal Cyndy Cannell dramatically reversed the fortunes of Webster Elementary School in Magna, Utah. She credits her success to her "KQS formula," applied to every program, activity, or encounter with parents, staff, or students:

    KEEP   What should we keep doing?

    QUIT   What should we quit doing?

    START   What should we start doing?

Hold Everyone Strictly Accountable for Performance

If managing for results is to make any sense, then the organization must hold every person in the organization accountable for his or her performance.

"We have what we believe is a noble mission," says the Salvation Army's Lieutenant Paul E. Bollwahine. "But unless one has a tight-knit organization, unless one has controls, unless one has ways of judging the quality and effectiveness of one's work, then no matter how noble the mission, the goals of that mission will not be achieved. We constantly have to check to see if what we're doing is as effective as we think it is."

At first glance, the Salvation Army seems a contradiction. Here is a religious organization whose leaders are ministers ordained in the Salvationist Church. Yet this is an organization that was founded to make war, one in which these same leaders hold military ranks and wear uniforms. Terms like *regiment*, *brigade*, *officers*, and *soldiers* are an integral part of its lexicon, and its official publication is titled *The War Cry*.

The Army began in 1865, when a Methodist minister named William Booth left his ministry to form an independent evangelist movement, the East London Christian Mission. Thirteen years later, Booth and his associates, meeting to transform the organization, announced, "The Christian Mission has met in Congress to make war. It has organized a Salvation Army." The army was to fight for the spiritual and moral regeneration and physical rehabilitation of those in need around the world. Today, more than 130 years later, the Salvation Army is widely regarded as the organization that, by converting outcasts into citizens, probably does a better job with the poor of this nation than anyone else.

Every year more than thirty-five million Americans and millions of others worldwide are assisted by one or more of the Salvation Army's array of community services:

- More than eight million individuals annually find shelter in Salvation Army housing facilities.
- The Army provides more than fifteen million meals a year, not counting those served in its rehabilitation centers and permanent residences.
- Ten million people a year receive material assistance from the Army.
- Millions of Americans, some 2,700,000 in 1996 alone, have benefited from the Army's emergency disaster services. When, for example, the tragic bombing at the federal government building in Oklahoma City took place in April 1995, Salvation Army workers were on the scene within minutes. In the first three weeks following the blast, more than 3,000 Salvation Army officers, employees, and volunteers rendered more than 61,000 service hours. These workers provided almost 104,000 items of food and drink to victims and rescue workers and arranged travel for family members and friends of more than 300 victims. In addition, Salvation Army personnel supplied counseling attention to more than 1,600 victims and family members.
- The Army conducts a host of youth programs, including scouting, boys' and girls' clubs, and camping programs that serve millions of young people every year.

- Millions of senior citizens are aided by the Army every year through such services as housing, health and day care, transportation, and recreational programs.
- The Army operates 145 rehabilitation centers that serve men and women addicted to alcohol or drugs. These centers, with an average capacity of ninety, are the cornerstone of one of the most effective rehabilitation programs in the nation.

Providing this level and diversity of assistance each year requires extraordinary efficiency. Lieutenant Colonel Beatrice Combs explains how this efficiency is based on management strategies developed by a single individual. "He researched, stated, described, and documented the problem," she says. "He defined his client group. . . . He listed goals and measurable objectives and described methods and programs. He set forth his theory and basic principles. He dealt with organization, management, research, and public participation. He did cost analyses, prepared budgets and timetables."

Tom Peters? Jim Champy? Peter Drucker? No, Combs was describing the work of Salvation Army founder William Booth as articulated in his book, *In Darkest England and the Way Out*, written in 1890. At the heart of Booth's blueprint for management was the call for a total dedication to accountability on the part of each individual in service to the Army. More than one hundred years later, accountability is still the Army's hallmark, institutionalized through fanatic devotion to an organizationwide system of checks and balances.

The Salvation Army's chain of command is clearly spelled out. National headquarters in Alexandria, Virginia, coordinates the activities of the four U.S. regional offices, which in turn oversee the activities of divisional headquarters in each state. The divisional headquarters have jurisdiction over local units. It is through the efforts of the approximately 10,000 local units that the real work of the Army is accomplished. Each unit has a community advisory board that oversees everything the unit does. The board, made up of representatives from throughout the locale, assesses the social needs of the community using three main criteria: (1) Is there a community need? (2) Can funding be obtained to meet that need? (3) Is the program under consideration in keeping with the Army's mission statement? Once these determinations are made, the board advises the unit about introducing new programs and revamping existing projects.

All of the local units are self-funded. They get their money from Christmas kettle collections, from direct mail solicitations, through allocations from the United Way, from government contracts for specific programs and from offerings and donations collected in the local church. "The heartbeat of the Salvation Army is the local unit," says Major Tom Jones, national secretary for community relations, "and the heartbeat of the local unit is its ability to fund programs to meet the needs of the community as clarified by its advisory board."

In addition to the checks and balances provided by its advisory board, each local unit is required to submit annual goals, five-year goals, and ten-year goals for review. All local units are also required to conduct comprehensive reviews of their finances, programs, and personnel.

Each divisional headquarters, in turn, comes under constant scrutiny from national headquarters, which conducts stringent annual audits of all programs, property, and operations. It all adds up to an accountability system that rivals the most stringent found in the business world, one that, according to Major Tom Jones, "never lets us forget that good intentions are not enough, that we're all responsible for everything we do and that our main purpose is to accomplish what we set out to achieve."

The Salvation Army's Cardinal Rules for Meeting the Bottom Line

The Salvation Army enjoys an international reputation as an organization dedicated to managing for results. Following is a summary of the organization's cardinal rules for "meeting unlimited needs with limited resources," as set forth by National Commander Robert A. Watson:

- Keep first things first. To put it another way, the main thing is to keep the main thing the main thing. It requires a constant reminder to everyone in the organization as to why there is a Salvation Army in the world and what its mission is.
- Maintain strict integrity in business. There should never be any question about that. Our word must be our bond, and anyone dealing with us should rest assured that there will be no misrepresentation, no shortcuts, no special interests or conflict of interests.
- People are important. The paperwork and administrative functions in this complicated age are more than burdensome. Sometimes they are overwhelming. Every person must be of immense importance to us. People are the reason for our existence. People are the focus of our mission. People provide our ministry and people receive it. The dignity and worth of every individual is recognized in Salvation Army service.

◆▸

The Salvation Army's Cardinal Rules for Meeting the Bottom Line
(continued)

- Stewardship is essential. We are to shun materialism and avoid greediness on the one hand. On the other, a prudent, careful allocation and use of resources is incumbent as we seek to spread limited resources to meet unlimited needs. Our cherished reputation for making a dollar go further than most other organizations must be more than a reputation. It must be demonstrated every day by our stewardship.
- Results are more important than plans. We are in a bottom-line oriented society. Salvation Army supporters want to know and have a right to know what results are being produced. It is important for us to be able to clearly identify families we have reunited and restored, wayward youth turned in the right direction, alcohol and drug abusers cured, liabilities turned into assets.

Organize to Act Quickly

The art of managing for results begins with planning. But planning must be backed up by a course of action and a willingness to act and react quickly. In The Nature Conservancy (TNC), for instance, it is what you do, not what you say, that counts. "Getting the job done is the critical thing," says former chief operating officer (COO) Bill Weeks. "That's always been the hallmark of the Conservancy." When the negotiating parties involved in TNC's acquisition of a 502-square-mile area in New Mexico finally settled on a sale price of $18 million, the Conservancy's board of governors conducted its telephone vote within hours, authorizing a $1 million down payment to secure the land.

The Natural Heritage Program was established to provide the scientific data for carrying out TNC goals. But it also gives state chapters the information they need to act swiftly on purchases. The telephone votes that authorize these purchases commonly take place less than twenty-four hours after a request is made. "We stand in line like anybody else to buy property," past president William Blair was fond of saying, "but we can act very quickly. We have often done a million dollars worth of business through a single phone call. All of our state chapters know that in order to purchase land that contains endangered plants or animals before developers can get their hands on it, that they have the authority to commit to the purchase immediately and that national headquarters will back them up."

Developing a bias for action includes creating an organizational climate in which responsiveness becomes a hallmark. At the Centers for Disease Control and Prevention (CDC), this means being able to respond within hours to a sudden public-health threat, an outbreak of disease, the eruption of a Mount St. Helens, or a chemical spill.

In the early days of the Salk vaccine, for instance, six inoculated children came down with polio. Within thirty-six hours, the CDC identified the cause as a single batch of vaccine from one laboratory, removed the tainted vaccine, and circumvented a potential panic that might have jeopardized the entire vaccination effort, which has gone on to eradicate the disease in a single generation. Responsiveness also entails dealing with changing public-health needs. Fifty years ago, the CDC focused on polio, smallpox, and malaria. Today, environmental hazards, injury prevention, youth and family violence, and AIDS are the agency's main concerns. Says former deputy director Walter Dowdle, "CDC is known for its ability to quickly marshal resources, to take on and complete a task. It is constantly changing or being challenged to change. It's difficult to become hidebound or rigid when you're interacting continuously with the public at large. For close to fifty years, people at CDC have become used to creating a new program within days, not years. And the agency is able to phase out and curtail things, too, to make resources available to do something else."

At the CDC, acting quickly also means facing mistakes squarely and rectifying them openly and as soon as possible. For most of its organizational life, the agency has been largely isolated from the kind of political winds that shake other bureaucracies, even its colleague, the National Institutes for Health. But it has not been free of controversy. Public impatience with delays in finding the cause of Legionnaires' disease and outcries over CDC findings regarding toxic shock syndrome and the effects of Agent Orange have shaken the agency. The agency's low point came in 1976, when the CDC discovered that a new flu outbreak in New Jersey was related to the deadly swine flu virus that killed millions of people in 1918. The agency recommended a nationwide effort to vaccinate as many Americans as possible. Fifty million Americans received flu shots against an epidemic that never materialized. More than a thousand Americans who got the immunizations later contracted Guillain-Barre syndrome, which has caused significant suffering to the victims and has cost the government $84 million in medical claims. The CDC survived the shock of this outcome by acting in a manner typical of the organization. It was the first to draw national attention to the problems its own recommendations created. It faced up to the controversy not by politicking or by laying low, but by dealing with the issue squarely and going on with its work with its integrity fully intact.

Acting Quickly

Some years ago, a small woman wearing a black dress, black hat, and black lace-up shoes and carrying a black umbrella appeared at The Nature Conservancy's national headquarters. Identifying herself as Miss Ordway, she asked to speak to the Conservancy's president, who was then Pat Noonan. The receptionist informed the woman that Noonan was not available and asked if she could help her. "I need to talk to the president about buying prairies and creating a prairie park," replied the visitor. Her statement got her the attention she sought. Noonan was quickly summoned and led her into his office.

"How much land did you have in mind?" he asked. "Oh," she replied, "as far as the eye can see, thousands of acres." As he continued to talk to his diminutive guest, Noonan discretely slipped a note to his secretary asking her to check out the identity of the visitor. A few minutes later, while Miss Ordway was reminiscing about growing up on the Minnesota prairie, the note was passed back to him. "She can pay for it," it read. "She's the heiress to the 3M fortune."

Within hours, the Conservancy launched a search for available prairie territory. Within days, it located 7,600 acres in South Dakota. Miss Ordway was immediately notified and, upon her return to the Conservancy's office, took out her checkbook and wrote a check for the full price of the land—$1,420,000.

Boost Results by Sharing Power

"People," says former deputy assistant secretary of defense Bob Stone, "want to do their job the best way they know how. And if you give them the authority to do their work the way they want to do it, they respond with enthusiasm and creativity and they do four times as much, four times better. It doesn't have anything to do with what you're paying them. They get a fair paycheck. But what people really want is to be in charge of their world."

Stone was the driving force behind the Department of Defense's Model Installation Program (MIP). The core of this unprecedented program was a one-page memo that replaced a telephone-book-sized volume of regulations. At the heart of the memo was the following directive: "The Commanding Officer of an installation is responsible for accomplishing the mission assigned to the installation, and should be delegated broad authority to decide how best to accomplish the mission, and is accountable for all resources applied to the mission." As Bob Stone explains, "For thousands of years, military people have known that's how they had to operate in wartime.

But applying this to the peacetime operations of the Department of Defense was revolutionary."

With the MIP in place, the Alameda (California) Naval Aviation Depot took the power-sharing program to heart and pushed it to the limit. The more than four thousand men and women at the Alameda facility maintained navy aircraft as well as engines and missile guidance and control systems. They also provided maintenance and engineering support to the ships home-ported in Alameda, California. Given the power to run their operations in the way they, rather than Washington, saw fit, Alameda's top management in turn pushed decision-making power down to the front line. "It's a real simple philosophy," says Rob Mixon, who ran the depot's paint shop. "We sat down with the foremen and said, 'Look, guys, that shop over there, that's your business. Those people that work for you, they're your stockholders.'" Mixon calls it a "let's do it" philosophy. "We don't sit back and say, 'Well, we don't think it's a good idea because it's not our idea.' We said, 'Let's do it. Let's see what happens.'" Mixon and his co-workers literally make every penny count. "We used to throw away a roll of masking tape when it was starting to get used up," says Mixon. "We started saying to our people, 'every inch of everything that's wasted goes toward the cost of this product. You're buying it. You're the stockholder. Now, do you want to waste it?'" Other depot teams were infected with the same spirit. One group of mechanics, for example, rescued a $30 million plane from the scrap heap by developing a way to splice a new nose onto the damaged aircraft. An engine technician found a way to repair previously scrapped combustion engine liners. His one idea saved the government (and the taxpayers) $11 million a year.

Power Sharing Can Supercharge Quality Improvement

Throughout the Alameda depot, employees took their decision-making power and put it to work not only on cost savings but on quality improvement as well.

With its emphasis on worker control and full participation, Alameda's Total Quality Management (TQM) movement was the engine driving the depot's astonishing turnaround. The landing gear TQM team at Alameda, for instance, made substantial changes by measuring and observing its own work process. It developed an inventory control system to better meet scheduling demands; designed and manufactured five containers to hold components during maintenance that prevented damage during handling; and developed a protocol for controlled disassembly to prevent unnecessary processing.

The most important event of the year at Alameda was the Zero Defects Luncheon. The title itself kept everyone's eye on the goal. At this luncheon, the winners of the Artisan and Service Achiever of the Year award were honored by the entire staff for their contributions to the productivity and effectiveness of the Alameda Naval Aviation Depot.

Before the MIP was initiated, Alameda's performance indicators placed it last in the navy's rankings of its six aviation depots. In just two quarters (180 days), Alameda's empowered workers had boosted their productivity and instituted cost-saving measures that enabled the depot to climb to number two, despite constant rumors that the Alameda base would become a victim of widespread base closings.

The Alameda turnaround challenges deeply held beliefs about government performance. "If there's one thing that irritates the life out of me," says the depot's former head of productivity planning, Dean Merritt, "it's the old saw, 'It's good enough for government work.' The workers at Alameda proved that when government people are given real authority, they can teach their counterparts in the private sector a thing or two about quality and performance."

The General Accounting Office was established in 1921 to serve as the federal government's accounting firm. It has evolved into an agency that, over the past two decades, has saved taxpayers tens of billions of dollars while leaving its footprints on most of the legislative and policy decisions made by the U.S. Congress. Along the way, it has built a reputation of rock-solid credibility even among the most relentless critics.

In its early years, the GAO took no responsibility for judging the wisdom of a particular expenditure, looking only at the legality of spending money on it. It was during Lyndon Johnson's administration that the major shift in the GAO's responsibilities took place. Elmer Staats, the comptroller general, convinced Congress that the agency, through the strict standards it already had in place, could evaluate government programs, report on their strengths and weaknesses, and issue recommendations on how programs could be most effectively pursued and improved. In 1967, a year after Staats took office, Congress asked the GAO to make its first major program evaluation—an assessment of such Economic Opportunity Act programs as the Job Corps and Head Start. From that point on, requests from Congress for GAO evaluations of government programs began to accelerate.

Because Congress depends on its work, the GAO has developed systems to ensure that its reports consistently meet the highest standards. Once the GAO receives a request to evaluate a program or an agency, that request is reviewed at least twice by the leadership of the relevant division and separately by the comptroller general and his senior management team: Is the assignment worth the resources needed to explore it? Is the right question being asked? Does the GAO have an efficient and reliable way of developing the data needed to answer the question? Is the proposed analytical approach likely to yield a valid result? Are the right people working on the assignment? Will the results be available in time to meet the anticipated need?

Every report that the agency issues is backed up by hours of planning, by consultations with experts in specific areas, and by the application of strict safeguards prescribed for every stage of a report's preparation. Throughout the preparation, oral briefings are given to every party that will be affected by the report—members of Congress, other agencies, and private-sector parties. An equally stringent set of standards is applied to the preparation of each oral testimony presented to Congress.

During the evaluation, there are continuous progress reviews. Congressional assignments involve frequent contact with appropriate Congressional staff to ensure that they are informed and that the requested work is still relevant to Congressional needs. At the draft stage, the GAO solicits comments from those affected by the agency's findings, conclusions, and recommendations. These comments are published as part of the final report. If the comments challenge the contents of the draft, the GAO staff analyzes and responds to them before the report is published, and this response is also published with the report. If, as sometimes happens, the agency under review provides additional information that was previously not available or points out flaws, the GAO reexamines its conclusions and recommendations. If the GAO decides that the other agency's arguments are valid, it makes an appropriate change before publishing the report.

In addition to reviewing each report in progress, the GAO also has a mechanism for systematically reviewing its evaluation process in general. An independent staff annually selects a sample of the agency's reports and examines in detail how the assignments were planned and carried out. Actions by the GAO staff are compared with the required procedures. Any deviations are analyzed to determine their cause and effect. The results are reported to the GAO's senior management both to reinforce the importance of the quality control procedures and to identify procedures that may need modification.

Says former comptroller general Charles Bowsher, "We have a motto around here that sums up our whole approach. That motto is, 'We control the signature.' We just won't let anything go out of here unless it accurately presents our objective evaluations, no matter what the ramifications."

Measure Performance in Customers' Terms

Managing for results entails continually measuring the effectiveness of both personnel and programs. The city of Phoenix, Arizona, constantly measures the performance of each of its departments based, in great part, on customer feedback. Each department files regular reports on its customer ratings, and the city publishes the results of a biennial survey of customer perceptions of service—hard numbers compiled by private, independent marketing firms. These surveys form the basis for Phoenix's corporate strategic plan, a plan dedicated to implementing clear, quantitative improvements based on what the city's citizen/customers tell it needs to be done. The survey also influences compensation. Each department head's pay is determined in part by customer ratings of the department's performance.

Personnel director Carlos Arauz has set strict standards for his department's customer service. No phone is allowed to ring more than three times before being answered. A call can be transferred only once. All calls from citizens must be returned within twenty-four hours. Logs are kept to document and measure performance against agreed-upon standards. Before the new service program was instituted, 58 percent of citizens felt that the department was doing an excellent job. Within five years, the rating soared to 98 percent.

When it comes to dollars-and-cents measures, Phoenix's audit department keeps an eye on every department's performance and documents its own in a detailed annual report. The economic impact of the 1995–96 audits totaled almost $1.5 million in savings or cost avoidance:

- Maximizing the volume of petroleum delivered in each fuel truck trip—$466,725 cost savings.
- Raising library fees to bring them in line with other libraries' charges—$2,500 increased revenue.
- A review of elevator maintenance billing found overcharge —$131 cost recovery.
- A review of solid waste bid collection process eliminated duplicate reporting process—$10,000 cost avoidance.

In the last five fiscal years, aggressive audits by this one department have put more than $13 million in spending power back into the Phoenix budget. Says city auditor Jim Flanagan, "We aren't auditing as cops but as productivity and service delivery consultants."

Innovation for Results

Phoenix's energy management section runs on entrepreneurial lines. Each year's budget is based on the value of energy savings generated the year before. It's no surprise that former department head Darshan Teji champions the cause of innovation. Here are his rules for promoting innovation for results:

1. Take the word *routine* out of your vocabulary.
2. Every day, everything is new. Learn. Be interested.
3. Never say, "Do this." Say, "This is the project. I don't care how you do it."
4. Keep your door open for problems. Otherwise, just wait for results.

Use Your Board to Maximize Your Results

There was a time when nonprofit organizations selected board members almost solely on their ability to give money to the organization and to encourage their friends to give as well. That is still one important function of any nonprofit board. But today, the best nonprofits know that they need much more from their boards. The board needs to monitor overall performance, keep management up to the highest standard, and help set policies and priorities. The best nonprofits realize that a board can be used effectively to provide what National Theatre Workshop of the Handicapped board chairman Rob Sennott terms "a reality check," a watchdog responsibility that, while not interfering with the day-to-day operations of the organization, holds management accountable for the performance of every worker, paid or unpaid. And effective nonprofits also know that they must constantly reassess the performance of the board itself, replacing those who have become burned out or too busy with other matters and recruiting others, particularly younger people, who can make important contributions.

The Nature Conservancy is guided not only by its national board of directors but also by boards in each of the fifty states—more than a thousand state board members in all. The Conservancy seeks out successful, business-wise individuals who are passionate about the organization's mission and then recruits them aggressively. National and state board members, past and present, include some of the country's most powerful chief executive officers. One of the boards' most important functions is to help raise funds. They also provide the political clout needed to acquire land in specific states.

The broad experience of board members is useful in other facets of TNC's operations as well. "Besides fundraising and access, we look to our boards," says director of member and partner communications Ron Gaetz, "for help in areas like communications where individual board members have particular experience and skills. And we look to them for guidance with particular issues. For example, when we first got into drafting an affirmative action plan, various members of our national board had all dealt with this issue and they were of immense help."

Greg Low, a TNC vice president, cites another specific kind of board member contribution. "We had a member of our California board, a real curmudgeon, who browbeat the staff about the importance of strategic planning. This was in the early seventies, a time when the last thing we wanted to do was plan. All we wanted was to go out with six-guns blazing and do the next land deal. As a board member can do, he insisted that we engage in some strategic planning. Well, our first attempt was awful. We came up with some kind of cookie-cutter plan that indicated that we'd just keep doing what we'd been doing. He insisted that we go back and do it again. So we went back and this time we really focused on considering both short-term and long-term goals. And we were surprised how important that was. We do it all the time now, but it was a board member whose insistence brought us to the table."

The entire Conservancy staff has learned a lot about how to work most effectively with this essential resource. "Your best board members are going to be your busiest people," states former Latin American director Geoff Barnard. "They're busy because they're good and everybody wants them. You've got to give them a sense of success. One of the mistakes I made early on was going to board members with vague and unfocused tasks for them to do. We'd have a board meeting and we'd distribute a list of seventy-five people or organizations that we were going after for money and would assign ten or fifteen of these to members present. They'd go off and be unsuccessful and not return my calls because they were embarrassed. Pretty soon I'd stop calling them and I'd lost them. Well, I learned. If I really needed to establish a meeting with an important potential donor or with a powerful person who could help us in some other way, I phoned a board member whom I knew could set up such a meeting and asked him if he'd do it. For him it was a simple task. He did it; he felt good about being successful, and I made sure that I thanked him for doing it."

The Board Team

Like their counterparts in the private sector, many public-service organizations are fond of using sports analogies to describe effective management approaches. Several years ago, the staff of the Children's Museum of Denver came up with the following list of nine major attributes that members of a board of directors need to possess, comparing these attributes to those that were key to the success of nine legendary baseball players.

First Base—Attendance and Participation (Lou Gehrig). For many years Lou Gehrig, perhaps the greatest first-baseman of all time, held the major league record for consecutive games played (2,130). Regular attendance and participation are necessary for all board members to fulfill their responsibilities to the organization. It's important that other board members and the staff are able to count on a board member's presence.

Center Field—Planning and Guidance (Joe DiMaggio). A center fielder sees the entire field, and no center fielder was better than Joe DiMaggio at seeing where his team needed to go and leading it there. Similarly, board members must have the vision of the entire organization in front of them.

Pitcher—Setting Policies and Establishing Goals (Sandy Koufax). Board members help govern the institution (not manage it) by setting policy and establishing goals for the management. Just as great pitchers like Sandy Koufax able to set a pattern of pitches throughout the game and set certain goals for pitching to batters, a good board member looks beyond day-to-day management issues toward the broader governance issues of the institution.

Left Field—Insurance (Ted Williams). Great batters provide insurance for the success of their teams. Ted Williams fulfilled his role as "insurer," and good board members should also understand their roles in seeing that their organization has adequate financing. Oftentimes this takes the form of direct fundraising. Other times a board member must guide the staff in fundraising efforts, just as Ted Williams guided the other players on his team and helped them become better hitters.

Second Base—Public Relations (Jackie Robinson). Not only did Robinson play at 110 percent at all times, but he also diplomatically and intelligently represented the Brooklyn Dodgers under intense pressure. Good board members must support their organizations with the same kind of commitment showed by Jackie Robinson.

Catcher—Selection and Evaluation (Johnny Bench). Johnny Bench selected pitches and evaluated the game as well as any catcher in history. Board members must carefully select and evaluate their chief administrator/

➤

The Board Team (continued)

---

executive director, and they must strive to become masters at working closely with executive directors, because it is the executive director who manages the organization.

Right Field—Accuracy (Roberto Clemente). Great right fielders like Clemente are known for the accuracy of their throwing arms. Good board members must attempt to be extremely accurate in their dealings with the organization and the public. One of the most important aspects of that accuracy is maintaining proper legal records and legal counsel.

Short Stop—Resourcefulness (Ozzie Smith). There was nothing in baseball more magical than watching Ozzie Smith perform one of his acrobatic feats. He always seemed to find a way to make the play. Good board members should strive to be as resourceful as Smith. They should be prepared to help supply the organization with advice, contracts, and whatever other resources are needed for success.

Third Base—Set the Pace (Brooks Robinson). Brooks Robinson and other great third-basemen have had the ability to change the pace of the game by moving in three steps or shifting their position ever so slightly. Those subtle movements can become effective tools for winning the game, and with the same subtlety board members can effect the pace of their organization, particularly by helping management and staff determine priorities and in what order they should be pursued.

Use the Books to Keep Score

Brother Rick Curry, founder/director of the National Theatre Workshop of the Handicapped, knows that money is a scorecard to help managers focus on results. "What I'm very proud of," he says, "is that, from the day I founded this organization until today, I can tell you where every penny has gone. I've always believed that if you're arrogant enough to announce to the world that you're here to help, you have to become custodian of all the money that's given to you. I firmly believe that anyone who gives you money has the right to come in and look at your books. If we fall flat on our faces, it will be because our time has passed or a calamity has fallen upon us, but it's not going to be because we didn't know how to handle what we've been given. Every theater group that has folded is probably as talented, if not more talented, than we are. The amount of talent here in New York is staggering. You can have a casting call for a six-foot-four-inch, *zaftig*, blonde young woman with one blue eye and one green and twenty are going to show up and they're all going to be loaded with talent. So why have we survived and others haven't? It's precisely because we have totally dedicated ourselves to credibility in regard to our benefactors. The secret of our success is financial accountability based on good, solid management."

Ellen Schall's Tips for Managing for Results

During her tenure as commissioner of New York's Department of Juvenile Justice, Ellen Schall established herself as one of the public sector's most effective leaders. Here are her tips for managing for results:

- Planning must go top-down, bottom-up. The top should plan the policy. The bottom should plan implementation.
- Get a long-term strategic agenda on the table while you're dealing with the short-term crisis. Continually ask where you want to be as an organization. Write a history of the future.
- Develop a reflective capacity. Ask what's going on, from which everyone can learn individually and as a group.
- Create effective forums. People need groups. They need to look across at people, not up or down.
- Support your staff; nurture and acknowledge them; catch them doing things right.
- Face mistakes and fix them. Place emphasis on pilots.
- Celebrate small wins.
- Get help early and often, but don't overrely on it.
- Acknowledge the hard stuff—the pain of work, the irrationality. Start with yourself, not with others. Understand that people will resist change.
- Create your own opportunities. Don't wait to be asked.

PART II

COMPETENCIES

This is the core of our study: a roster of strategies by outstanding organizations to achieve top performance. As we spent time speaking with managers and staff on-site and observing little pieces of structure, behavior, and approaches, we documented more than two hundred separate, practical strategies that made these organizations better than average. As we examined our findings more closely, it became clear that, numerous as they were, these strategies fell into seven clearly definable areas of competence that enable the most effective public and nonprofit organizations to meet and embrace the challenges defined in the first section of this book.

We were surprised to discover that our seven competencies echo in number those put forth by Tom Peters and the McKinsey Consulting Group. But there are important differences. We found effective partnerships to be the lifeblood of several of the organizations we studied. We also found that the unabashed, relentless selling of the organization's product or services—something not usually associated with government agencies or nonprofits—was common to top performers.

These, then, are the categories that evolved from our findings, competencies that will be documented by example throughout the remainder of this book.

Serving the customer. All these organizations understand that they exist first and foremost to serve their customers. They know their customers, live for them, and display an insatiable curiosity about them. They survey those they serve, spend as much time with them as they can, and, whenever possible, bring them directly into the organization's operations. They have all come to know that different customers need and want different things, and they keep the lines of communication open so they can constantly assess and reassess their priorities.

Sharing the power.   All of the organizations we cite have pushed power down the line and out from headquarters. Employees work harder and more efficiently in these organizations because they are put in charge of their own operations. In most public agencies and nonprofits, those with the most direct knowledge rarely have the power to put this knowledge to work. The organizations we studied demonstrate that giving decision-making power to those closest to the action is one of the most direct routes to organizational effectiveness.

Valuing people.   The organizations in this book know that their people are their greatest asset. They are characterized by the value they put on their employees, the trust they place in them, and the respect they show them. This is evident in the emphasis placed on training everyone in the organization in both job-related and personal skills. All of these organizations invest heavily in celebrating their people and find innovative ways of rewarding them.

Creating a climate for innovation.   In a rapidly and radically changing economy, every organization has been forced to find new ways of doing things. The government agencies and nonprofits we studied make a science of constant innovation. They solicit new ideas from everyone. They listen to each idea and act quickly upon those that make sense. They recognize and reward contributors for ideas that work, and they encourage everyone to examine other organizations for good ideas to "swipe." Most important, they make innovation a hallmark of everything they do, from creating new programs, to finding ways of increasing their resources, to rewarding their people, to serving their customers.

Forming effective partnerships.   Most of the organizations we studied leverage their resources through partnerships. By joining forces with outside partners, these organizations bring in new financial and human resources and fresh ideas. They have also discovered that the most effective partnership arrangements are those in which the partners share equity, responsibility, and authority—in which each partner experiences a true sense of ownership and is constantly recognized for its contributions.

Selling the product.   We were surprised that many of our organizations go out into the market and aggressively sell their products and services. Again, that is not something one usually associates with government agencies and nonprofits. But as we revisited our organizations, we discovered that for them "selling the product" was not only an important management approach; it was a key to their success.

Communicating effectively.   Our vanguard organizations make communication a priority. They understand that communication is the glue that holds an organization together. They know that in today's decentralized organization, characterized by autonomous teams, constant and effective communication throughout the organization is a key to top performance. The most effective organizations encourage formal and informal mechanisms for sharing ideas and concerns, achievements, and even failures. Most have established cross-departmental teams not only for efficiency's sake, but to make sure that each department knows what the others are doing. Several have introduced courses in listening skills into their training programs. And some are beginning to make a concentrated effort to get the good news out to the public. They are all characterized by the way they have established a culture of talking, listening, encouraging curiosity, and information sharing.

4

SERVING THE CUSTOMER

When it comes to customer service, nonprofit and public organizations operate under severe handicaps. First, they don't get their funds from customers. The people who pay for the services of the Salvation Army or the General Accounting Office rarely use the services directly. This distance from the quick feedback of the market can land an organization in trouble. It has earned the government a reputation for being slow moving. Nonprofits have been scolded more than once for providing endowed services that no one uses. In fact, government and nonprofits don't necessarily suffer when demand for their services dries up; but they can suffer when consumer demand rises.

Second, most public agencies and many nonprofits provide services that cannot be obtained anywhere else. This profoundly complicates the operating environment. Dissatisfied customers can't take their business elsewhere. Agencies can become complacent, slow moving, and openly contemptuous of customers, knowing they're the only game in town.

The third and most challenging handicap is the tension among the many customers and constituents of these organizations. This tension is familiar to commercial businesses, who also serve many customers. The makers of dog food have to please the dog, the owner, and the supermarket owner and manager in order to succeed in the marketplace. The difference in the case of government and nonprofits lies in degree and in the involvement of the community at large as customers. To return to the maker of dog food for a moment. That business rarely has to deal with outraged olive oil customers who feel that dog food is taking up shelf space in the market that rightfully belongs to them. Nor does the dog food maker have to hold public hearings on whether the manufacture of dog food is an appropriate use of limited foodstuffs. Yet these conflicts with the community at large regarding mission or policy are familiar to many managers of government agencies and nonprofit organizations.

Consider the members of a local school board, for instance, or the board of a nonprofit school. This board must serve many customer groups, each with different demands and expectations: the community, neighbors, teachers, parents, students, and—in the case of a public school district—taxpayers. Government agencies routinely serve many groups. For instance, the Department of Housing and Urban Development must serve builders and developers to make sure housing gets built, low-income families who live in the housing, the communities in which public housing is located, and citizens at large. A moment's thought reveals that each of these groups will have a different concept of the role of public housing in a community and the level to which such housing should be funded, to name only two volatile issues. Nonprofits, too, must perform the same kind of balancing act. The Nature Conservancy, to cite one example, serves many groups: environmentalists and other life scientists, business and government organizations, and landowners, all with different interests in the land and animals.

Finally, a single customer of a nonprofit or government agency can have multiple *and* conflicting demands. As Tom Peters has pointed out, when a citizen wants to build an addition to her house, she wants responsive, streamlined government, but when her next-door neighbor wants to add to his house, she wants a government that moves slowly and includes everyone, especially neighbors, in the decision process. As a citizen concerned with the environment, you probably applaud when a nonprofit organization like The Nature Conservancy buys up a large tract of land to preserve it from development. But if you're a developer, a builder, or employee in a related industry, you probably don't look upon the action so favorably.

The ideal of superior customer service has helped build and expand many businesses, large and small, but does customer service have a place in government and the independent sector? How can you define a standard of service that can be delivered to customers with conflicting needs?

In our investigations, we found dozens of organizations that provide superior service for all their customers, whose commitment to customers has helped them survive and prosper, and whose customer service skills are equal to any in the corporate world. In the following pages you will encounter the strategies that these organizations employ for reconciling conflicting customer demands and building superior service. These strategies are built around the following concepts:

- Customer service begins with knowing who your customers are.
- Every contact with a customer is critical.
- Customer service demands heart as well as brains.
- Customer service demands guts as well as brains and heart.
- Customer service is enhanced when everyone truly participates.
- Maximize your customer service by putting people before programs.
- Treat everyone like customers.
- When it comes to customers, no standard is too high.
- True customer service transforms customers.
- Customers should be brought into the action.
- Listening to customers is essential.

Customer Service Begins with Knowing Who Your Customers Are

Set in the foothills of Magna, Utah, with mountains and the Kennecott mining operations as a backdrop, the Webster Elementary School was part of the Granite School District, Utah's largest. Located just south of Salt Lake City, Granite covers some 300 square miles, with eighty-nine schools that serve almost 76,000 students.

The Webster Elementary School, which served a community with a high percentage of low-income, single-parent, and minority families characterized by high mobility, stands as a shining example of how a local community—with the help of an inspiring and dedicated leader but without any special advantages or additional resources—can turn an average local school into a model school where learning is exciting, challenging, and fun. (Although Webster has since closed because of problems with an old classroom building and its students have been dispersed to other schools, the lessons of its success are still relevant.)

Principal Cyndy Cannell led Webster's turnaround. When Cannell arrived in 1985, she found an environment characterized by high teacher turnover, frequent vandalism, and discipline problems. Parent involvement was very low and student absenteeism alarmingly high. On her second day as principal, Cannell broke up a gang fight involving eighteen youngsters.

In very short order, Webster became a totally different place, with clean and bright classrooms and playgrounds. Bulletin boards announced a growing number of school and community activities and events. Student attendance rose dramatically. "My main goals," says

Cannell, "were to improve the self-image and self-esteem of the students, to make them want to come to school, and to make them proud of the fact that Webster was their school."

She began by addressing basic issues. When there was an outbreak of head lice at the school, she recognized that it presented an embarrassment for students and their families. So she did the screening herself in order to guarantee student confidentiality. "Cyndy personally screened all of our four hundred kids," says Webster parent Kay McDonough, "and she followed through and rescreened. She educated parents through handouts and slide programs."

Cannell also set out to reduce vandalism by building students' pride in their school. She got students involved in planting a "pride garden" with flowers, vegetables, and fruit trees donated by local merchants. "It is important," says Cannell, "to help children appreciate their community and to understand how vandalism brings down their school."

Perhaps Cannell's greatest contribution to the Webster turnaround was the way in which she conducted a concerted campaign to let her teachers, her staff, and all those around her know that Webster parents were to be regarded as real customers, just as important to the success of the school as the students. She realized from the time her tenure began that one of her first goals had to involve breaking down the barriers between parents and the school. She knew that the major contributing factor was that many of the parents had suffered negative experiences in their own schooling. She began inviting parents to the school, making them feel comfortable and sharing with them ways they could help their youngsters feel better about themselves through their educational experience. "We immediately got to know parents by their first names," says Cannell. "I introduced myself to every new parent and told them how pleased I was that their child was at the school." Once she began gaining parents' confidence, she concentrated on getting them actively involved.

Cannell obtained state training in school policy and budget matters for members of the PTA board. She then gave the board input on all school policies and nonconfidential issues. She encouraged all her teachers to contact parents with progress reports on their children at least once a month and requested that parents, in turn, submit monthly "report cards" on the school, which she reviewed and acted on. Parents became increasingly involved. They even assisted Cannell in applying for foundation and government grants, which eventually supported a summer lunch program and a computer lab. Says Kay McDonough, "When Cyndy first came to Webster there was no PTA organization and total volunteer hours for the year were 159. Before her work at Webster was completed, there were more than 3,000 volunteer hours, and we were chosen as the outstanding local elementary unit in Utah by the national PTA."

Like an MGM movie, the San Diego Zoo (officially, the Zoological Society of San Diego) traces its beginnings to the roar of the lion. In 1916, when the Panama Pacific International Exposition closed its doors on its final visitor, it left behind a motley collection of lions, wolves, monkeys, and deer. Driving home one night, Dr. Harry Wegeforth, a leading citizen, heard the unlikely roar of a lion in the city's park and decided that San Diego should have a zoo. So he started one.

The San Diego Zoo is one of those rare organizations that has been a success from its very beginnings. In 1922, with three miles of brand-new fencing surrounding its facilities, it began collecting a ten-cent admission fee. Within four years, 30,000 visitors a year were pouring onto its grounds, and several new construction projects had begun. Throughout the 1950s and 1960s, the nationally syndicated television program *Zoorama*, accompanied by the regular TV appearances of goodwill ambassador Joan Embery (and her exotic animals), brought the zoo to the attention of the nation.

Today, employees of the zoo care for about 4,000 animals of 800 species. The spectacular Wild Animal Park, which was established in 1972, contains more than 4,000 animals of some 285 species. The zoo also houses an extraordinary plant collection gathered over the years from all corners of the world. In addition, the Zoological Society operates the Center for the Reproduction of Endangered Species, which among its many activities in behalf of wildlife reproduction contains a frozen zoo that houses tissue samples of some 350 endangered species. Its purpose is to preserve these tissues in the hope that some day technology will allow the cloning of animal life from tissue cells—especially those species that by then might be totally extinct.

The management and staff of the San Diego Zoo are quick to proclaim that the driving force behind their many achievements is their commitment to customer service. As director of marketing Martha Baker told us, "There is no way we could compete against such blockbuster operations as Disneyland and Sea World if we weren't so fanatic about making sure that the needs of every visitor are met as completely as possible." Martha Baker is the one in the hot seat. Because the zoo dedicates itself to earning its own way without government money (or the strings that come attached), marketing at the zoo is just as serious as it is at Honda or Pepsi. Baker and her staff realize that they have to come up with different marketing strategies for different kinds of customers. There are the millions who come to the zoo each year to view the animals and the astounding plant collection. There are others who have an interest in supporting the zoo's conservation and scientific activities. As Baker says, "There's increased interest in the environment and the conservation ethic, but there are a lot more organizations competing for public attention. People who support us are often making a decision to switch away from supporting something else like The Nature Conservancy, so we have to make sure we know who they are, what their interests entail, and we have to tailor our marketing strategies to let them know we can meet those interests."

Families make up the greatest segment of the zoo's visitor population, and in the intense competition for families' leisure dollars Baker keeps a close eye on demographic trends. "People are taking shorter vacations and are staying closer to home," she says. "Not as many families as in the past are traveling across the country to visit San Diego or the zoo." Baker and her staff carefully segment markets within their area, targeting San Diego first and then Orange and Los Angeles Counties through direct mail campaigns, coupons, and group sales to the military, corporations, and associations. And the zoo has a tradition of long-term market building. Every year it brings every second-grade class in San Diego to the zoo for a special, bang-up tour.

Every Contact with a Customer Is Critical

Most taxpayers have no idea if the navy is building the right number or the right kind of nuclear subs. We have no way to judge how efficiently the Department of the Interior, the CIA, or even the state house are being run. But we sure know when our garbage isn't picked up on time or when the fire department is slow in responding to our call. Citizens come face to face with government at city hall. Phoenix, Arizona, has nurtured this closeness, increased citizen-customer contact, and become one of the best-managed cities in the country. While customer-driven government may not draw tourists or make for pretty postcards, it has enabled Phoenix to meet the challenges of both growth and recession and has enhanced the quality of life for citizens.

Phoenix was incorporated more than a hundred years ago and became a city in the years following World War II. In 1940, it encompassed only nine square miles, with a population of some 65,000. Today, it is the seventh-largest city in the United States, with a population of more than one million living in a 469-square-mile-area.

With the beginning the population boom in the late 1940s, Phoenix reorganized its troubled and corrupt municipal government. A new charter set clear and limited powers for an elected mayor and city council while placing the management of government in the hands of a professional city manager. That's how Phoenix still operates. The mayor and council, as elected representatives, set policy and priorities but, the professionals manage the day-to-day business.

In the 1950s and 1960s, reform continued with programs for careful budgeting, accounting, planning, and performance measurement. Through the 1970s and 1980s, productivity reforms, performance auditing, zero-based budgeting, and performance-based compensation for middle and top managers were introduced. Today, as municipal governments across the nation are forced to cut programs and question every tax dollar spent, Phoenix is in better shape than most. It meets challenges with a tradition of high performance and accountability, innovation, employee participation, and exceptional customer service. In 1993, Phoenix won Germany's Carl Bertelsmann Prize as the best-run city government in the world. (Phoenix was the only U.S. city in the candidate pool, and the only city with a population of more than 500,000.)

Phoenix operates like a holding company with twenty-four departments that oversee enterprises as varied as conducting elections, paving streets, fighting crime, repairing machinery, collecting garbage, developing and managing real estate, and putting out fires. Each department has a separate mission and separate performance standards. They are united under the city's general mission and overall high performance standards.

Of these overall standards, first and foremost is customer service. Wherever we went in Phoenix, we met municipal employees who were thinking and talking about their citizen-customers. Even those who didn't serve the public directly talked about ensuring that their functions would help other Phoenix employees serve the customer effectively.

Phoenix personnel director Carlos Arauz runs a department responsible for processing and testing applicants for city jobs. In 1990, the department had 110,000 applicants for 1,500 jobs. Arauz sees his department's job not as a gatekeeper, controlling access to a limited resource, but as a facilitator, helping as many people as possible to be successful in their applications. "When you think about it," says Arauz, "it's not surprising that many people have negative attitudes about city government. Most people come into contact with city government through the courts, the police, and the personnel department. Their experiences with the courts and with the police are not always pleasant. We have to make certain that citizens' contacts with our department are positive. It's a real challenge."

"When you can only hire 1500 people out of some 110,000 applicants," Arauz points out, "you're going to have more than 98,000 disappointed citizens. So it's critical for this department to manage each customer contact in a way that ensures that they know they are being treated fairly. We do everything we can to make sure that this happens. We answer all questions courteously, help each candidate through the application process, and treat everyone with respect. If an application is denied, we make certain that the candidate is given timely and valid reasons for our decision."

Personnel's customer service training program has now been adopted by twenty-four other city departments. Participants have come up with some innovative ways of serving Phoenix citizens better.

- In the water and wastewater department, employees adopted flexible work hours so they could extend telephone and information counter hours into the evening for the convenience of citizens.
- Street transportation department employees developed door hangers to put on citizens' doors to alert them to upcoming street maintenance and repairs. The hangers inform residents of scheduled start and finish dates so they can plan their routines to minimize disruption.

Customer Service Demands Heart as Well as Brains

The Phoenix fire department is one of the busiest in the nation. In 1995, it answered 122,850 emergency calls. It's also one of the most efficient departments of its kind, with an average response time of three-and-one-half minutes. Chief Alan Brunacini jokes that his people's dedication to serving their customers costs the department about $35,000 a year. He's referring to the fact that, in their haste to respond to a call, fire crews occasionally race through the firehouse doors before they are fully open.

The men and women of the Phoenix fire department know that their job entails more than just responding quickly and successfully to emergencies. Compassion is an essential ingredient in the way the department's paramedic units operate. Once they've sent a citizen to the hospital in the fire department ambulance, paramedics at the scene put the furniture back in place and pick up bandages, syringes, and wrappers. It is a matter of customer service—and heart. They don't want a family to return home from the hospital to more reminders of the trauma they have suffered.

Fire department employees are always looking for more and better ways to serve. During the first five months of 1989, eleven children in the Phoenix area drowned. The fire department turned the situation around by establishing seven Drowning Adaptive Response Teams (DART) of specially trained paramedics to respond as quickly and effectively as possible to drowning accidents. The department secured foundation funding and developed a program to educate the public about drowning prevention and emergency medical treatment. Within a year, thanks to this "Just a Few Seconds" education program, the number of emergency calls for drowning accidents had dropped from 101 to 48.

Maintaining the Commitment

In its commitment to maintain its reputation as a customer service organization, the city of Phoenix continually adds to its roster of services. The city has made it easier for citizens to do business in a number of ways:

- Building signs that previously contained bureaucratic-sounding department names have been replaced by signs that list services and functions.
- Most government agencies list their departments by official name in the blue pages of the telephone directory. This is useful only for those citizens who know the name of the department whose services they are seeking. As with the building signs, Phoenix has begun to list its departments in the telephone book by the specific services they provide.
- The city established a concierge desk at the Phoenix Convention Center to direct and assist conventioneers.
- New ten-minute parking zones outside of the Convention Center box office make it easier for customers to purchase tickets.
- Expanded hours and an improved reservation system for the city's ball fields make arranging games easier.
- Special listening devices installed in various departments assist hearing-impaired citizens.

Customer Service Demands Guts as Well as Brains and Heart

Phoenix's Public Works Department provides a prime example of how far the city will go to serve its citizen-customers. In 1978, in the wake of various revenue-reducing propositions passed throughout the nation, Phoenix decided to put refuse collection out to bid. Soon after this decision was made, Mayor Margaret Hance asked public works director Ron Jensen if he intended to compare the incoming bids from private companies to what his department costs had been in providing the service. Jensen responded, "Yes, and we're going to enter into the bidding ourselves."

By entering his city department into direct competition with private companies, Jensen was putting his own job on the line while developing an entirely new brand of privatization. Yet he believed that going head to head with the private sector would force public works to learn some tough lessons about streamlining and efficiency. He was convinced that if the department learned those lessons, it had a good chance of winning the bid.

To make the process absolutely fair, Phoenix's city auditor had his department certify public works's bid, using the department's records to allocate fairly the costs of equipment, labor, and other expenses. Jensen, in fact, never saw his department's bid until all the bids were opened.

In the first two rounds, the city was outbid by private-sector collectors. "But," says Jensen, "we saw the productivity that private companies were getting from their more sophisticated equipment—larger trucks, advanced lift systems—and we borrowed these ideas and incorporated them into our next bids." In the process, his entire department also became expert at checking costs and chargebacks from other city departments. They learned to pinch every penny, even reducing and reorganizing the department in order to find savings without diluting their services. In the third round, they won the bid. "Before contracting out," says Jensen, "there was little pressure on our department. We had nothing to compare our performance against; there were no real incentives. Now employees have been seized by a competitive spirit." And, he might add, the cost of refuse collection to the taxpayers has dropped an average of 4.5 percent yearly.

Based on the successful Public Works Department experience, Phoenix has now put a number of city services up for competitive bidding, including landfill operation, street maintenance, water-meter repair, building cleaning, bill processing, park concessions, ambulance and paramedic services, and some security services. In open competitions from 1979 to 1994, city departments won twenty-two contracts while private companies won thirty-four. The bottom line is that, no matter who wins the contract, it's a win for Phoenix. As of June 1996, the city auditor computes that public/private competition has saved Phoenix taxpayers $18,010,800.

Customer Service Is Enhanced When Everyone Truly Participates

Beth Israel Deaconess Medical Center, a major health care facility in Boston, Massachusetts, is a winner in the most competitive industry and the most competitive market possible. The fact that both doctors and patients consistently rate it tops keeps it in business and gives the hospital an international reputation.

Beth Israel Hospital was established in 1916 to serve Boston's growing Jewish immigrant population. The original hospital contained 45 beds, and was staffed by 23 physicians. The first official act of the hospital, founded to care for those who often felt unwelcome at other facilities, was to declare that its doors would be open to persons of any race, creed, nationality, or economic circumstance.

In 1996, in the face of major hospital mergers that were taking place in the Boston area, Beth Israel completed a major merger of its own, combining forces with Boston's Deaconess Hospital. The new organization, called Beth Israel Deaconess Medical Center, became a subsidiary of a newly formed parent corporation called Caregroup Inc. Unlike many other merged hospitals, Beth Israel Deaconess operates with one board of trustees, one administration and management, and one set of chiefs for its clinical services and departments.

Thanks to the merger, the medical center has 673 beds and 56 newborn bassinets and is staffed by more than 5,025 people, including some 1,145 physicians and more than 1,320 registered nurses. Beth Israel Deaconess treats about 40,000 inpatients and some 360,000 outpatients a year, while some 49,000 people annually receive treatment in the emergency room.

Long before its merger with the Deaconess, Beth Israel (BI) had established a solid reputation as a leader. It was BI that first developed the cardiac pacemaker. It was BI that first published a formal statement on the rights of patients. And BI led the industry in implementing an employee-based participative management program. But according to the medical community and those whom it serves, it has been BI's extraordinary commitment to customer service that sets it apart from most health care facilities. Likewise, superior customer service has also been what set Boston's Deaconess Hospital apart. (Its motto has been, "Where science and kindliness unite.") Above all else, it is customer service that distinguishes the newly formed Beth Israel Deaconess Medical Center.

"This is a major teaching and research facility and we're proud of our reputation," says Dr. Mitch Rabkin, former BI president and now CEO of the medical center's parent organization. "That's the high-tech side of what we do, and we have to work hard to maintain our standards. But at the same time, we have to realize that we are dealing fundamentally with people, and in an environment of high technology, the human issues are increasingly paramount."

At Beth Israel Deaconess, customer service is everybody's business. The medical center's roster of customer representatives includes not only doctors and nurses but also custodians, security personnel, and housekeepers. They all know that it is part of their jobs to make patients and their families as comfortable as possible. In many hospitals, for example, a person can wander around for a full day without anyone acknowledging her or offering help. At Beth Israel Deaconess, if someone is wandering around looking confused, any employee will volunteer to help—and that employee will probably escort the person personally to her destination. "Whether it's walking a wife or daughter to the garage," says the medical center's patrol manager Charles Grant, "or helping a nervous new dad get

the keys out of his locked car, as long as patients know that someone is here helping the ones they care about, they'll rest a little
easier. I think a hospital is one of those places where a little can
mean a lot." Says senior maintenance mechanic Steven Raus, "As
someone with a mechanical engineering background, I'm in a
unique situation at the medical center. The human element makes
my work so much more rewarding. I'm not here to just produce
widgets; I'm here to help people. The training I've received here to
become more sensitive to patient's needs has made a huge difference in how I see my job."

That Beth Israel Deaconess truly cares about its customers and
that it institutionalizes this caring is further evidenced in countless ways. For example:

- In addition to providing regular paid television services to
  which all patients can subscribe, BI Deaconess operates its
  own closed-circuit television station. Originating from the
  facility's video production center and made available free
  of charge to all patients, the medical center's Channel 3
  carries health-oriented educational programs that provide
  practical tips on health care, covering a wide variety of
  subjects. Every half hour there is a brief station break featuring a member of the BI Deaconess family—a doctor, a
  nurse, a maintenance person, a housekeeper, a meal deliv-
  erer, a volunteer—who speaks to the patients about his
  or her role in the hospital and concludes by urging them
  to "Be well!" These spots are designed to let the patients
  "meet" those they see every day while they're at the hospital, an important method of letting patients know that
  everyone at Beth Israel Deaconess is interested in making
  good customer care possible.
- Youngsters accompanying adult clinic patients or visiting
  inpatients receive an official "doctor's kit" in the shape of
  the familiar doctor's medical bag. It is filled with cartoons,
  drawings, puzzles, and games introducing them to the types
  of people they'll see at the hospital and what they do. It
  describes the types of experiences their relatives will have
  at the hospital, and it's all designed to make a child's visit
  to the medical center less frightening and mysterious than
  it otherwise might be.
- Beth Israel Deaconess maintains a concierge service that
  provides information about restaurants, museums, sight-
  seeing tours, and the like to family and friends of patients
  who are undergoing inpatient or outpatient surgery. Beep-
  ers are given to these relatives and friends so that when the
  surgery is completed, they are immediately notified and can

return to the hospital or phone the doctor. The concierge service also maintains a business center where those waiting for a relative or friend to come out of surgery can plug in their laptops and occupy their time while awaiting news from the doctor. All of the people who operate the concierge service, including its director, are volunteers.

Beth Israel Hospital's Statement on the Rights of Patients

In 1972, Beth Israel Hospital demonstrated its concern for its customers by issuing its now-famous statement on patients' rights. Here is a synopsis of this statement, which has been adopted by hospitals around the world.

- You have the right to receive the best medical care for your problem regardless of your race, color, religion, national origin, or the source of payment for your care.
- You have the right to be treated respectfully by others and to be addressed by your proper name and without undue familiarity.
- You have the right to privacy.
- You have the right to seek and receive all the information necessary for you to understand your medical situation.
- You have the right to know when students are to perform specific examinations or treatments that pertain to your care.
- You have the right to leave the hospital even if your doctors advise against it, unless you have certain infectious diseases that may influence the health of others, or if you are incapable of maintaining your own safety, as defined by law.
- You have the right of access to your medical record.
- You have the right to be free of the effects of the smoking of others.
- You have the right to inquire about the possibility of financial aid to help you in the payment of hospital bills and the right to receive information and assistance in securing such aid.

Maximize Your Customer Service by Putting People before Programs

In America, metropolitan centers set the trends: fashions from New York and Los Angeles; social experiments from Denver and Miami; theorizing from inside the Washington Beltway. But in a tiny town called Sunbury, a special group of trendsetters has pioneered a new way of puncturing the bloated bureaucracy and delivering social services better, faster, cheaper, and more effectively than ever before.

Sunbury is located in Northumberland County, a 453-square-mile, pork-chop-shaped piece of east central Pennsylvania. Many of the 100,000 people in the county work on farms or in food processing factories. Incorporated in 1772, the county last hit the national news when Sunbury's city hotel became the first public building in the nation to be wired for electricity under Thomas A. Edison's personal supervision. Right across the street from the scene of Edison's triumph is the County Department of Human Services' Children's Clinic, an agency that is bringing Northumberland to national attention again.

The Children's Clinic was the brainchild of Mike Breslin and arose out of his frustration with the bureaucratic barriers to getting troubled youngsters and their families what they needed when they needed it. In 1985, Breslin, head of the county's juvenile justice system, was appointed to the dual position of director of mental health and mental retardation services. He viewed his expanded role as an opportunity to push forward a bold new experiment. "I found myself," he says, "in a position to make the mental health system behave differently." The Children's Clinic, which he established in 1987, is a customer-driven team process for getting help to troubled kids and their families as quickly and as effectively as possible. Its strength lies in the way it draws on every one of the county's human services, as well as the local schools, without requiring any additional financial resources or personnel. The secret of this agency's success is that it has been able to smash age-old bureaucratic barriers by asking, "What does this child and family need?" rather than "What do we have to offer? or "What funds does Juvenile Justice have to offer?"

Every Wednesday afternoon, the Children's Clinic brings together representatives from every agency in the county's Human Services department. The representatives sit down at one table with a troubled child and his or her family to work out a treatment plan for the youngster in need. (The Children's Clinic representatives are not necessarily agency heads; they come from various levels of their departments. For the purpose of the Children's Clinic meeting, they are all designated "liaison staff.") No one leaves the table until a realistic plan for helping the youngster is devised, the resources to make it happen are identified, and the customers have agreed to the plan. Representatives of the various agencies commit resources on the spot. There is no waiting for bureaucratic authorization.

It sounds like an ordinary, sensible way of arranging matters, but it is not the way things used to be done in Northumberland County or, for that matter, are still done in most of the 2,800 counties in the United States. "Prior to the Children's Clinic," explains Breslin, "when a kid got in trouble in the courts, school, or wherever, a case worker would do an assessment. If that person decided drugs and alcohol were the real problem, then the kid was passed over to that agency, where they did another assessment and drew up a treatment program. But if they wanted to call on another agency's resources, then the case was usually tossed over the wall again and a third assessment was done. By the time that actual help got to the kid and family four to six weeks would go by. The immediate crisis was over, and the family had lost hope or interest."

Bringing together customers and staffers from various county departments and giving the staffers equal footing, decision-making power, and a vested interest in the outcome of each case has gone a long way to making the Children's Clinic a model of thrift and efficiency. Despite difficult economic times, the range of services provided by the clinic has actually increased. An independent study has revealed that the Children's Clinic's innovative approach has decreased the need for expensive, out-of-home placements in the county by 20 percent. Most important, the citizen-customers of Northumberland County feel that the clinic is doing a better job for them. Says county resident Flo Berry, "When I walked into the clinic everyone at the table knew what I was there for. They had done their homework and they were prepared to help. The role of everyone involved was explained to me and I felt from the start that everything I said was important to them. They explained the different programs that were available that my son would benefit from. I left there feeling that I wasn't the only one in the world who had a problem with a fourteen-year-old son and that something would be done." Says former Northumberland County juvenile probation officer Charles Chervanik, "The Children's Clinic is the one government agency I know of that has reduced expenses while providing greater services."

Treat Everyone Like Customers

Along with serving troubled youngsters, their families, and the schools, the Children's Clinic has come to understand that its customer base is larger than originally envisioned. "We came to realize that the community at large is our customer," says Mike Breslin. "Those of us in social work who came out of the sixties saw ourselves as advocates for the person at risk, and we set ourselves up as adversaries of the broader community who we saw as the noncaring enemy. We did ourselves and the people we served a disservice. We learned that our customers are not just the individuals, families, and youngsters we serve, but our customers also include the police department, which looks to us for solving a problem, the hospital, even the chamber of commerce, who come to us because they're concerned about something they see in the community. And by creating a culture of listening and cooperating, of working with other service agencies rather than competing with them, we developed a countywide system in which everyone realizes that they are important customers of each other."

True Customer Service Transforms Customers

America's nonprofit sector is one of the nation's unique strengths. As the late management expert Bruce McGhee once reminded us, "Only the nonprofit sector is capable of taking a dime's contribution and turning it into a dollar's worth of service to the community." Independent-sector organizations often perform another kind of magic by bringing together ignored, threatened, or victimized segments of the population and serving them as well as Federal Express serves its customers.

Everything that the National Theatre Workshop of the Handicapped (NTWH) undertakes, from theater courses to playwriting competitions to student performances, is driven by the deep commitment to meet special needs in a special way. "We train our students for the marketplace, not just the theater," says the organization's founder, Brother Rick Curry. "That's because when you train a disabled person to become articulate, you're making a better salesman. We're giving our people the courage to go after the next job interview. There's that stupid myth that one should hire the disabled because they're always reliable. The reason we look so reliable is that we're terrified to lose our jobs. And so we'll come to the same job for forty years because we don't think we have the wherewithal to better ourselves. You want to know some of what my triumphs have been? It was when one of our blind students came to class and she'd had her hair done. It was when another student quit her job and went out to look for a better one. It was when another student went to his boss and told him that he'd like to chair the next departmental meeting. He did it, did it well, and got promoted. Those are all genuine triumphs." Sensitivity to students' needs includes an understanding that standards must be high and never compromised. "Believe it or not," says Brother Rick, "we spend a lot of time teaching reading skills. If you're cute and disabled in school, you get away with murder. So a lot of our students simply don't read well. If they're blind, we don't let them learn their lines through electronic recordings or devices. We insist that they use Braille and we teach them to read it well. And that's transferable."

Says Louis Lo Re, the NTWH's former managing director, "NTWH is an organization that has never compromised. That would not serve its students. They find out right away that lateness will not be tolerated, that anything less than professionalism has no place in this organization." Adds Brother Rick, "We confront our students and we help them accept who they are, how they can celebrate themselves. We teach them that acting is much more an exercise in undressing than in putting on costumes. And when they start to understand that, then that's when you begin to have an actor."

Bring Customers into the Action and Involve Them at Every Stage

"Customers are at the root of our values," says Paul Richard, Children's Museum of Indianapolis's executive vice president. "Our visitors are the stakeholders in this place and are seen as partners in every aspect of our work." The design and development of every new exhibit, activity, or set of materials starts and proceeds with the kids. The museum's largest gallery, for example, its innovative, hands-on Eli Lilley Center for Exploration, was designed almost totally by youngsters.

Placing such power in the hands of its young customers is not always easy. "I'll be summoned to a meeting where the kids are presenting their ideas for a new exhibit," says Peter Sterling, the museum's president. "I'll listen and sometimes I'll think that what they're proposing is just awful. But I'll bite my tongue and let them proceed. We test each new exhibit or activity with the public before we formally put it into place. But I can't tell you how many times the kids have come up with something that I didn't think would work that has turned out to be one of our most popular and effective creations." Says one young member of the museum's Youth Council, "We know what kids want better than the staff does. We know what works with kids our age."

The Indianapolis museum's volunteer staff is made up primarily of its young customers. "As our volunteer staff," states Sterling, "we use interested kids, feed them, cultivate them, give them apprenticeships, and they become the best teachers of other kids. We have 650 young volunteers. The parents drive them or put them on the bus to get here. And day by day they demonstrate that they're our most important volunteers."

"We have real participation," explains one of these young workers. "We don't just show people around. We're at the exhibitions all the time and we see what works and what doesn't. When we suggest a change, the staff really listens. It's the volunteers that make this such a great place. We can do things with visiting kids better than anyone else."

At the museum, customers speak up and expect to be heard on *every* subject. "One of our most important incidents took place on a day when a group of our youngsters was meeting with thirty scientists and marketing people from Dow Chemical," states Paul Richard. "Up to that point Dow had been a contributor to the museum but had not participated in any of our activities. As soon as this meeting began, one of the kids asked the man who had invented the zip-lock bag why Dow was producing something that could not be disposed of safely. The Dow people promised they would begin to research ways to deal with this problem, which, by the way, they have done. Most important for us, this one incident made us examine our policies and led to the recycling program we have put into place."

Listen to Your Customers and Let Them Define Their Needs

Bringing customers into the operations of a children's museum is one thing. Bringing customers inside a large urban police force is something else again. Nonetheless, the Baltimore County Police Department has achieved remarkable success by policing *with* its community.

Located in the heart of industrial Maryland, Baltimore County covers 610 square miles and surrounds, but does not include, the city of Baltimore. The county has a population of over 700,000, including, as one of its officials noted, "the richest of the rich and the poorest of the poor." Its governmental structure is unusual; none of the many towns in the county are incorporated. The 2,000 men and women of the Baltimore County police force have the sole responsibility of providing police services for the entire county.

Violent crime had never been an issue for citizens until a six-day period in the summer of 1981. On August 10 of that year, a twenty-two-year-old man was murdered as he opened his family's sporting goods store in a neighborhood shopping mall. Five days later, a sixty-one-year-old citizen riding his moped was shot and killed by two men driving by in a stolen car. Frightened citizens formed neighborhood vigilante patrols and victims' rights groups. Stories of crime dominated county newspapers. The county executive and the county council released funds to hire forty-five new police officers.

Ironically, just a few days before these crimes took place, Chief Neil Behan had attended a seminar that documented how the fear of crime, more than crime itself, can decay a citizen's way of life. Behan decided to find out how fear affected his own constituents. He had his officers interview hundreds of county citizens. They discovered that many of those surveyed were frightened of going out at night, opening the door when someone knocked, walking past a stranger, being in bank or supermarket parking lots, and calling the police or signing a complaint as a witness or victim of a crime. Armed with this information, the chief decided on a bold new plan. He would use the forty-five new officers to free up forty-five specially selected and trained officers for a new kind of police operation designed to fight fear in the community.

The chief appointed a project team comprised of commanding officers to formulate the makeup of this new community-oriented fear-fighting operation. After a series of planning sessions, the team designed three units, each with thirteen officers and two supervisors. Each unit was assigned to one of the county's three patrol areas and was given its own quarters in an area precinct house. To distinguish these units from the rest of the force and to make them more accessible to the community, it was decided that they would give up closed-in police cars and would ride motorcycles. They gave the new force a name—COPE (Citizen-Oriented Police Enforcement).

COPE units were assigned to spend all their time out in the community, finding out what citizens perceived as the problems relating to crime. "When I graduated from the police academy," says Colonel Don Shinnamon, who headed the COPE units, "we, as police, defined the problems in the community through a slavish dependence on crime statistics. That's how all police forces worked and that's how most operate today. When COPE went into a problem area, we talked to the customers, we conducted formal surveys with everyone we could, and we talked informally with everyone we could to discover what was on their minds, what they believed were the problems. Businesses throughout the private sector continually conduct surveys to determine what the customer wants. But it is a revolutionary approach to policing. Cops don't do surveys; it's not been part of police work. There was a tremendous payoff to this approach. For what we found time and time again was that the problems were not what we thought they were. Police everywhere have always worked long hours and put in tremendous effort. What COPE allowed us to do was to direct these efforts where they were needed the most."

There was another important payoff to the community policing approach as well. "Normally, when the public comes into contact with a police officer," says Sergeant William Kahler, "it's at a time of stress—they're getting a traffic ticket, their house has been robbed, things like that. As a COPE officer, I spent almost all my time interacting with the men, women, and children of the county in a positive way. We truly got to know each other and they came to see that I was interested in knowing what their fears and problems were and in finding ways to correct them. Most important, they stopped seeing me and my fellow officers as a threat. There were long-term benefits to that not only for COPE but for the efforts of the entire police department."

In ten years, COPE exceeded the most ambitious expectations of its creators. According to an independent study conducted by Dr. Gary Cordner of the Criminal Justice Department of the University of Maryland-Baltimore County, COPE's strategy of directly involving those it serves produced these results:

- Reduced fear of crime by 10 percent in target communities.
- Reduced incidents of crime by 12 percent.
- Reduced calls for police service by 11 percent.
- Increased citizens' awareness of police presence by 20 percent.
- Increased citizens' satisfaction with police performance by 16 percent.

Ironically, COPE's success eventually put it out of business. In 1994, according to plan, COPE units were disbanded and COPE officers were assigned to every precinct, where they continue to practice problem-oriented community policing and to show fellow officers how they can "cope," too.

The main issue, as Chief Neil Behan defined it, continues to be "how can we improve the quality of life in our communities so that people can live in peace and harmony. That's what COPE is all about. There'll always be those who question whether taking police officers out of patrol cars to interact with citizens and to bring government and the community together is really our job. Well, if it's not our job, whose job is it? If there's no one else to do it, then it's our job."

Fundamentals of Effective Customer Service

We asked staff members from the city of Phoenix, the Government Accounting Office, Beth Israel Deaconess Medical Center, and the Northumberland County Children's Clinic to list for us what they regard as the essentials of effective customer service. Here is a composite of their lists:

- Make certain that serving the customer is at the core of your training program. Train everyone in effective customer relations, particularly in effective communication with customers.
- Create an organizational climate in which everyone is responsible for customer service. Make it clear to everyone that every contact with a customer is critical.
- Know who your customers are and what they're up to. Stay ahead of the curve by appointing interdepartmental teams to research and report on new trends and new demographics that could affect the nature of present or potential customers.
- Instill the understanding that no two customers are alike. Create written profiles of your customers. Share this information throughout the

Fundamentals of Effective Customer Service (continued)

organization and appoint teams to create new ways of meeting customers' special needs.

- Create opportunities to obtain feedback from customers. Survey them,
invite them to participate in training, visit them regularly, and, above
all, listen to them carefully.
- Don't withhold information from customers. Share the good news and
the bad. If you have a service delivery problem with a particular customer, invite that customer to help you solve it. You'll be surprised at
the way most customers will pitch in.
- Whenever possible, create partnerships between your organization and
its customers. Partnerships provide an opportunity for the various groups
to get to know each other better and to build trust.
- Place decision-making power in the hands of those closest to the customer. Give front-line people the authority to resolve customer problems immediately.
- Find ways to let customers know you appreciate them. Communicate
with them often and make sure these communications create opportunities for customers to tell you what's on their minds and to offer suggestions for improvement.
- Let everyone know that customers are more important than projects.
Make sure your organization asks, "What does this customer need?
rather than, "What do we have to sell to this customer?"
- Credibility and integrity are your organization's greatest assets. Never
deliver any service or product to your customer that is not of the highest quality. Don't promise what you can't deliver.
- Don't go for customer satisfaction. Aim for delight. You can never do
too much for your customers.

The examples we've just presented demonstrate that the most effective organizations know that serving the customer is their main
reason for being. They also understand that being customer-driven
means being active participants in the marketplace, and that when
you value and live for your customers, you are in the business of
sales. As we'll see in the next chapter, "sales" is really another term
for being there for your customers—communicating with them
continually, assessing their needs, and, wherever possible, bringing them directly into the action.

5

SELLING THE PRODUCT

During our investigations, we made some exciting discoveries. One of the biggest came as a blinding flash of the obvious one afternoon after we had completed what we felt was truly our final list of basic competencies shared by all the organizations we had chosen.

As we were discussing—for what seemed like the thousandth time—this list of competencies, we became aware that we had overlooked one big factor: Many of our organizations owe their effectiveness and even their existence to the manner in which, in one way or another, they sell their products or services. When we say "sell," we are not talking about marketing or customer awareness. We mean that the men and women of the organization are in touch with such terms as "samples," "competitive advantage," and "closing" and are not reluctant to practice foot-in-the-door, Fuller-brushman techniques.

Perhaps we should be excused for having overlooked the results of our own research. Most commercial businesses rise and fall on their ability to sell. Every day, information in one form or another comes back from customers about what they like and what they don't like and what they'd be willing to pay for. Nonprofits and public agencies, on the other hand, traditionally have labored under the terrible disadvantage of not selling. They beg or fundraise or even appropriate or lobby, but typically they don't go out to the men and women who use their products or services and try to sell directly to them. Most have no way of determining the value of their organizational efforts in cash. Even more important, they don't get minute-by-minute feedback on what and how they're doing.

Many of the organizations in this book do *not* insulate themselves from selling. Rather than stay out of the marketplace, they roll up their sleeves and wade in. They may sell to corporate sponsors as well as clients, but they approach both as potential customers with a clear understanding of what they offer and how the customers will benefit. They talk features, benefits, cost, and price. They talk competitive strengths. They anticipate customer objections. They talk relative value. And they don't take no for an answer. When they find the front door closed, they crawl in the back window.

Suppose, for example, you go to a fundraising event for a local park, where you meet a number of local environmentalists. One harangues you about the importance of saving the park, accusing you of being unaware, uninvolved, and uncaring. A second environmentalist takes you on a guilt trip by stating that the parks need so little while you have so much. While you are whipsawing between guilt and shame, a third person approaches. This person talks quietly about the benefits of saving the park and then gives concrete examples of various ways that people in the community have supported the effort—some through outright gifts, some through small payroll deductions, some through donations of time, some through a variety of other relatively painless ways of helping. The first two approaches, along with the preparation of grant applications, represent time-honored fundraising methods. The third approach represents a true understanding of sales.

But it is not just outstanding nonprofits who understand the importance of selling their product or services. It is no secret that government agencies historically have not felt the need to market their services. Where else are citizen-customers going to go to get a building permit, a driver's license, or a passport? Yet, as you'll discover in the pages that follow, there *are* government agencies like the Seattle Waste Utility that, like the nonprofits we studied, have developed specific strategies for selling face to face, tailoring their pitches to the customer, being entrepreneurial, being bold and aggressive, and using variety and perspective.

Don't Treat Selling as a Dirty Word, Treat It as a Way of Life

"There are two ways of approaching fundraising," states National Theatre Workshop of the Handicapped's founder, Brother Rick Curry. "You can line up all your ammunition and write grants for seed money. Or you can take a broom and push. I take the broom and I push hard. I know that federal money is drying up, and I never want to be in a position where I depend upon it. I've seen too many groups get federal money and then get cut off and die. Most importantly, you can't build an organization on today's money. You can only build on tomorrow's money. So you have to plan; you have to devote the time—and you have to push the broom."

Brother Rick has become devoted to a daily fundraising regimen. "The chairman of my board," he states, "is a salesman. He says you can't go to bed at night and rest your head peacefully on the pillow unless you've asked somebody for money that day or set up an appointment to ask them for money the next day. He says you have to ask ten times for every time you hear a yes. So if you don't make ten calls during a day, you're not going to have a funding source the following day. So it's always—always—push, ask, sell. Push, ask, sell."

Getting the Check

Dr. Harry Wegeforth was the founder of the San Diego Zoo, an organization that from its beginnings has been characterized by an innovative and successful approach to raising funds. There was the time, for instance, when Wegeforth approached a local magnate and asked him to underwrite the cost of a new elephant. The wealthy citizen cavalierly rejected the plea, saying that the only kind of elephant he'd pay for would be a white one. When the elephant arrived at the zoo, Wegeforth had him dusted with flour and led him to the magnate's house. Man and pachyderm left with a check.

Good Sales People Never Stop Selling

The National Theatre Workshop of the Handicapped (NTWH) is characterized by the way in which it seizes every sales opportunity. One of the architects of the NTWH's sales strategies was former managing director Louis Lo Re. "Everyone at NTWH," he says, "truly believes that they have a great product, better than anything of its type that can be found anywhere else. That's why they can all sell."

"You do everything you can," says Lo Re, "and you grasp every opportunity you get. It's a matter of networking, networking, networking. You can sit down and fill out an NEA grant form that weighs four-and-a-half pounds that will bring you in perhaps $25,000. A board member, on the other hand, can pick up the phone, make a call to a colleague, and get you $25,000 in ten minutes. Networking is the key to everything. You network with your board, your staff, your students, with everyone. You can't go to any function and not have your business card ready and your spiel all prepared. You never know who you're going to meet. You network cocktail parties, awards ceremonies, funerals—everywhere. You then go to your board and your staff and tell them about a person you've met. Do they know anything about that person? How can he or she help us? Does that person have a brother or another relative that might help? You send out these feelers because there's always a connection somewhere."

Lo Re's sales philosophy has become a way of life at the NTWH. When staff members are not selling, they're looking for opportunities to sell. They identify potential donors through foundation books, through the *Wall Street Journal*, and through the various business magazines. If they see in the *Wall Street Journal* that a company has had an incredible quarter, then they immediately pursue that company for funds. If they discover that someone they have pursued in the past has been promoted to a higher position, they pursue that person again. Recently they began writing to computer companies, letting them know how much they've improved the quality of life for the disabled by allowing them to do so much work at home. They let these companies know that there are forty-nine million disabled out there and suggested they run an ad showing a person in a wheelchair performing solid work. This approach is based on the philosophy that if they can't get money from a company, perhaps they can get publicity. If they can't get either money or publicity then perhaps they can get work for their actors.

NTWH'S Cardinal Rules of Fundraising

- Get it into your head that no matter what else you do, fundraising has to be a full-time occupation.
- Do your homework. Read *Town and Country* (a wonderful source for who is funding what), the society columns, the *Wall Street Journal*, the *New York Times*, *Fortune*, *Business Week*, *Forbes*, and every other newspaper and magazine you can get your hands on. Find out who the important CEOs and philanthropists are. They are all potential donors.
- Make sure you go to social events, cocktail parties, annual dinners. Know everything you can about potential donors who will be there. Where did the CEO go to school? Who is his wife? What does he own? What is his stock selling at? Who is working with him on a possible merger? Remember, you can't just be charming; it won't do you any good. You have to have a hook and it has to be at your fingertips.
- When you read about a new CEO being appointed, send a congratulatory letter. If you read about someone receiving an honor because of his or her contribution to some other group, send that person a letter of congratulations also. You never know when it may pay off.

●→

NTWH'S Cardinal Rules of Fundraising (continued)

- If you approach a funding source and encounter a lack of interest or find that the company's guidelines have changed, have three or four alternative projects at your fingertips, ready to present.
- Get to know the members of your board really well. Find out what other boards they sit on. Try to get them to help you tap into these other organizations for funds.
- Exploit your staff members and their contacts. Check your staff's alumni notes and college bulletins; they can be a real source of potential funders.
- When someone commits to giving you money, get it as soon as you can. People's business fortunes change; they get divorced; they die. Have a legal document ready for signing the moment a person gives you a "yes."
- Make sure that you properly acknowledge those who give you money. Unless they have objections, include them in your publicity. Invite them to your events. Send them birthday and Christmas cards. Inform them of good news whenever you get it.
- Above all, remember: sales is 85 percent work; 10 percent memory; and 5 percent luck.

Make Your Pitch Face to Face

When Rick Curry approaches foundations or corporations for money, he doesn't just send a letter or file an application, he mounts a personal sales campaign. "I push as hard as I can to get a personal meeting with one of the organization's officers," he says. "I've found that nothing will happen unless there's face to face contact. Once I'm at this meeting, I look at the person across the desk and I say to myself, 'Is this someone who likes business talk? Is this someone who I think would really rather talk about the goals of my organization and what we're accomplishing? Will he or she be impressed by the success story of one of our students or by the list of celebrities with whom we work?' What it really comes down to is my being a psychologist. I try to intuit how to break down the barriers, get that person to listen and to want to help us."

Once Brother Rick has captured a potential donor's attention, he then addresses what he regards as the most important issue—what his organization can do for the potential funder. "I always know how the funder can help us," he says. "They can give us money. But creatively I have to figure out if we can benefit their work and their mission and how I can articulate it to that person across the desk. It's a real process of scratching each other's back.

We have to understand that if we have nothing to offer the funders then we have no chance of being funded by them."

The Nature Conservancy (TNC) is a true fundraising giant. It raises some $14 million yearly from over 550,000 dues-paying members. Its biggest sources of funds by far, though, are the gifts of money and land (over $129 million annually) that are acquired from corporations and private donors. The reason that the Conservancy far and away outstrips its competitors for corporate and private donations is that, like the National Theatre Workshop of the Handicapped, it sells by outlining the benefits to donors.

"The Conservancy," states S. Bruce Smart Jr., former chairman and CEO of the Continental Group, "doesn't say, 'We're good and you're bad' to business; it says, 'Look, here's something that needs to be done in the interest of everyone. Here's how you can help getting that done in a way that will benefit you.' It's a balanced style that very much appeals to business executives." Adds *Industry Week*, "Among environmental organizations, The Nature Conservancy is unique. It's attracting increasingly greater corporate contributions because business feels 'comfortable' with it. A non-confrontational approach is a major reason—but when the Conservancy wants a particular piece of land, look out."

Tailor Your Pitch to the Customer

In its pursuit of every possible funding dollar, The Nature Conservancy continually comes up with a wide variety of ways that individuals and organizations can give to the Conservancy. At the heart of its "pitch" is a detailed, practical explanation of how the donor, as well as the Conservancy, will benefit from each particular type of donation.

Gifts of cash.   Many gifts to public service organizations are made by check. The Conservancy reminds its donors that cash gifts, when itemized on a tax return, are generally deductible up to 50 percent of adjusted gross income.

Gifts of stock.   The Conservancy encourages its donors to be tax-wise and contribute a gift of stock that has been owned for a number of years or stock that they have held for more than one year and that has increased in value. By making a gift of the stock, the donor avoids paying a capital gains tax on its increase in value. The Conservancy also explains that the charitable contribution deduction is equal to the full fair-market value of the stock, which is generally deductible up to 30 percent of the donor's adjusted gross income.

Gifts of real estate.   According to the Conservancy, a gift of real estate can also be tax-wise. A residence, vacation home, farm, or vacant lot may have so appreciated in value through the years that its sale would incur a sizable capital gains tax. By making a gift of this property instead, the donor avoids the capital gains tax and receives a charitable deduction for the full fair-market value of the property. The Conservancy conducts a staff site inspection of all real estate before it is accepted as a donation. If the property provides a critical habitat for rare and endangered species or ecosystems, the Conservancy then endeavors to provide for appropriate protection. If the land is not ecologically significant, it is considered a trade land gift. Trade lands are sold, and the proceeds are used for natural area protection elsewhere.

Retained life estate.   This strategy invites donors to give their homes, farms, or vacation homes to the Conservancy, while retaining the right to use the property for their lifetimes. Such a donor receives an income-tax deduction once the property is deeded to the Conservancy.

Life income gifts.   The Conservancy suggests various ways in which donors can make life income arrangements that allow the donor to increase her or his income, receive a charitable contribution deduction, and avoid capital gains tax, all while supporting The Nature Conservancy. Donors are urged to donate stock or real estate through one of several gift arrangements that provide a 5 percent or greater annual return. The income is paid to the donor and/ or a loved one for life, after which the principal is used by the Conservancy. These suggested life income arrangements also include:

- Long-term income funds, under which a donor's gift is pooled with those of others to achieve the highest sustainable yield.
- Charitable gift annuity, a contract with The Nature Conservancy that pays the donor a set quarterly payment for his or her life.
- Deferred gift annuity, an arrangement whereby a donor receives an income-tax deduction at the time of the gift, but payment to the Conservancy is deferred for at least one year.

Bequests.   The Conservancy points out that donors can give gifts to the organization through their wills. They can name The Nature Conservancy as the direct beneficiary of specific assets, a portion of an estate, or a residual estate after payment of other bequests. These bequests are entirely free from federal estate tax.

Retirement plans.   Under this arrangement, donors name the Conservancy as a beneficiary for part or all of their Individual Retirement Plan (IRA), Keogh plan, 401(k), 403(b), or any other qualified personal plans. The proceeds of these plans are distributed outside of probate and are entirely free from federal estate tax.

Formula for Success

In the process of acquiring millions of acres of land in order to save hundreds of species of endangered plants and animals, The Nature Conservancy has made more deals in more ways than Donald Trump, in his heyday, every dreamed of completing. Following are the precepts that TNC's top management regards as the keys to any organization's success:

- Make allies out of those who would traditionally be regarded as antagonistic while holding on to more natural supports.
- Give those closest to the action the responsibility and the authority to pursue and creatively structure the deals.
- In areas where you can't go it alone, build partnerships with those who can help make it happen.
- Recognize that the members of your board are free, high-class talent. Recruit a board that will allow you to tap into the best mix of managerial skills and experience. Assign specific, attainable tasks to board members. Allow them to succeed and they'll be there the next time you need them.
- Money talks, everything else walks. If you're involved in a deal, move aggressively. Don't delay. A good plan carried out today is better than a perfect one executed in a month or so.

Be Entrepreneurial and Make Selling Your Lifeblood

During its first three years, the Children's Museum of Denver operated solely on the basis of whatever grants it could obtain from traditional funding sources. In 1976, on the same day that a new executive director, Dr. Richard Steckel, took over, the three grants that made up the museum's entire operating budget expired. Rather than panic, Steckel set about developing a whole new approach to keep the museum alive and to assure its future. He decided that the museum had to take charge of its own destiny by weaning itself from its dependence on grant funding. He was convinced that the key was in establishing a continual flow of earned income in partnership with corporations that, for their own good business reasons, would fund the museum's many programs, exhibits, and activities. He targeted publishing for children and families as an area in which the museum could responsibly—and profitably—contribute.

Specifically, Steckel established an approach based on the following five principles, which guided the museum in all of its entrepreneurial activities:

1. *Preselling.* The museum never risked its own money in producing a product or event. It never undertook a project or event until funds to cover the full cost of production had been acquired from a corporate partner or partners.
2. *Wholesaling.* The museum never sold retail to the general public. Instead, it wholesaled its products to a corporate partner, which, in turn, distributed them to its customers. This approach cut down on the full potential of sales, but it allowed the museum to avoid "sitting on" unsold inventory and brought it guaranteed revenues.
3. *Pricing.* Prices for all museum products and events included three components: the direct cost of producing the project; the indirect (or overhead) costs of producing the project; and a profit.
4. *Diversification.* The museum believed that income diversification is healthy and that no project should ever provide more than a quarter of the organization's budget. It pursued many projects at one time, scheduled, as much as possible, to provide a steady cash flow throughout the year.
5. *Quality.* Quality counts. The museum's corporate partners respected museum staff as experts in family education. They were not involved in project development. The museum generally invited partners to look at a book or exhibit during development, but quality control rested strictly with the museum.

Be Bold—Don't Be Afraid to Be Aggressive

A dedication to selling and an ability to take on new products are not qualities usually associated with government agencies. Yet several of the effective government organizations we looked at are characterized by the way they have made selling a vital part of their management arsenal.

In fact, it is a government agency, the Solid Waste Utility (SWU) of Seattle, Washington, that is our candidate for selling champion. In early 1987, Seattle faced a serious crisis in its waste disposal operations. Both of its landfills were ordered closed. Mandated cleanup costs were estimated at $100 million. For a time, the city negotiated stopgap measures, but rising costs of the cleanup of the old landfills and landfill fees for the use of temporary sites raised the individual customer's waste disposal rates a whopping 82 percent.

It was clear that a fundamental redesign of Seattle's method of waste disposal was necessary. In 1988, the Solid Waste Utility, under the leadership of Diana Gale and with the support of the mayor and city council, launched a recycling program whose goal was to recycle or compost 60 percent of the city's total waste by

1998. "We knew that was an aggressive goal," says Seattle's senior recycling planner, Ray Hoffman, "but we knew it was necessary. From the beginning, those of us at SWU have operated under the theory that without an aggressive goal, there's no compelling reason to strive. Moderate goals call for moderate behavior."

Diana Gale attributes the essential success of this program to one major factor—the city's success in selling its new product. "The technical challenges of solid waste disposal," she says, "are child's play compared to the challenge of getting people to volunteer to change their habits. The reason for our success is the way we've been able to market our services by making citizens aware of the importance and the benefits of our program."

In Selling, Persistence and Variety Pay

The SWU's recycling efforts have been characterized by the aggressive and persistent manner in which the utility has sold citizens on the value of the program. Staffers and volunteers go out into the community, preaching the benefits of recycling and gathering information from citizens on what is working and what needs to be improved. They speak regularly at community groups to encourage participation and solicit citizen feedback. The SWU has become a small publishing house, creating and distributing scores of practical guides on every aspect of recycling, from composting to the effective disposal of household chemicals.

In addition to pamphlets and brochures, the SWU has also published recommendations for schools on implementing recycling education and has worked with the schools toward making courses in recycling a part of the curriculum. The utility also guides and supports Friends of Recycling, a citizen group that works with neighborhoods and other community groups to bolster the recycling effort.

In its efforts to reach all citizens, the SWU pursues every avenue and approach. Here are just a few of the ways they sell the program to Seattle residents:

- direct mailers to all customers;
- inserts in utility bills;
- door hangers on all residences;
- information flyers delivered with new recycling and refuse bins;
- attendance at public meetings and community events;
- trained customer service staff members manning SWU telephones for extended hours to answer customer questions;
- close relations with the media, fostered by press releases, weekly updates, press conferences, and media events for project milestones;

- training for key staff in press and public relations;
- continual market research about what customers want.

All of these selling efforts have paid off handsomely. The agency has "closed" with more than 85 percent of the city's residents, who are voluntarily participating in one or more of the city's various recycling projects. "We've received a lot of credit for the way we responded to a common municipal crisis," says Diana Gale. "It's something of which we're very proud."

Selling Change

Change is perhaps the toughest sell. When Diana Gale took over as head of Seattle's troubled Solid Waste Utility, she and her staff organized themselves to sell the citizens on changing their habits and making recycling part of their routine.

Gale identified these strategies as fundamental to selling change:

- Develop both short-term and long-term visions. Identify what success looks like today and what it will look like next month or next year.
- Focus on small starts and small gains. Long-term success will be achieved through a step-by-step process.
- Build teamwork. The more people with new skills and viewpoints that you can bring to the task, the better the chance of success.
- Encourage creativity. There are no packaged programs to help sell change. There are no models or well-trodden paths to the goal. Use pilot programs to test new sales strategies, to generate new ideas. Ask customers what would influence them to change.
- Establish oversight mechanisms. Monitor what is working and what isn't. Make necessary adjustments without delay.
- Communicate constantly with staff and customers. Communication is the single most important element in selling change.

Tips from the Selling Champions

We asked officials from The Nature Conservancy, the National Theatre Workshop of the Handicapped, and Seattle's Solid Waste Utility to list for us what they regard as the essentials of selling. Here is a composite of their lists:

- Operate with the understanding that effective selling is a full-time job. Devote a part of every day to raising funds. Be willing to accept rejection, knowing that for every "yes" you receive, there will be at least ten "no's." ➥

Tips from the Selling Champions (continued)

- Selling really means more than just fundraising. If organizations or individuals can't give you money, explore what other resources they might be willing to donate, including free publicity, human resources, or a list of other contacts.
- When you go after a specific organization or group for funds, begin your efforts by carefully researching the purpose, goals, and operating procedures of that organization or group. Tailor your fundraising pitch to show how your organization can specifically help meet their needs or objectives. (In sales, this is called qualifying a customer.)
- Train all your employees to understand that, in public service, "selling" is not a dirty word. Develop an entrepreneurial spirit within your organization by demonstrating how a bold approach to marketing your services and products is, above all else, an affirmation of the confidence you have in these services and products.
- Wherever possible, make full-fledged partners out of those to whom you wish to sell services or products. This strategy will minimize your risks while giving your partners a vested interest in what you deliver.
- As in fundraising, tailor the services and products you wish to sell to a particular customer to meet that customer's specific needs and objectives.
- Put quality first. Deliver the best services and products you possibly can, and chances are you'll get the repeat business your organization needs to flourish.
- Be in constant touch with those you serve. Survey them and respond to their questions immediately. Develop as many ways as you can to make contact with them.

Every successful organization has learned that, today more than ever, finding new resources is the key to best serving its customers and fulfilling its mission. For government agencies, this often means entering into collaborations that bring needed manpower and expertise. For nonprofits, it also means finding partners with the financial resources that are the lifeblood of the organization. As we'll see in the next chapter, operating effectively within these partnerships represents whole new ways of doing business.

6

FORMING EFFECTIVE PARTNERSHIPS

In the changed economy of the nineties, belt tightening isn't going to be enough. Businesses are responding to increased competition with serious layoffs (euphemized as downsizing or rightsizing) and massive restructuring. Nonprofits and public agencies are facing the same tough realities.

Over the past two decades, nonprofits have come face to face with harsh new challenges as traditional sources for workers—paid and unpaid—have dried up or shifted. At the same time, financial grants to nonprofits from government and private sources have shrunk or disappeared completely. Severe budget reductions and widespread taxpayer revolt have forced government agencies (federal, state, and local) to tackle more with less.

The best public-service organizations have demonstrated that maintaining quality service while spending less is not a matter of percentage cuts across the board. They have learned that they have to *restructure* to leverage existing organizational resources and to marshal new ones. This ability to develop and channel new resources is key to the success of many of our vanguard organizations. And the key to marshaling new resources is the ability to form collaborations with other entities in both the public and private sectors.

Current management gurus are talking about the new "virtual organization," which orchestrates collaborations across institutional borders. But these collaborations, under the name partnerships, have been in existence for a long time. In fact, partnerships in the public sector are as old as our nation itself. The federal government was not set up to operate independently.

Partnerships may actually come more naturally to government and nonprofit organizations than to their private-sector counterparts because successful, enduring collaborations must be built on a solid foundation of shared values and principles. The most effective partnerships we've found among public-service organizations are those that are not based merely on contracts, joint commissions, lobbying alliances, or even cooperative programs targeted at a common goal. Rather, they are collaborations that involve *long-term commitments to developing and implementing new ways of achieving those common goals.*

Building an effective partnership is not easy. Finding a partner or partners whose values, principles, goals, and ways of working are compatible can be a long and difficult process. But the potential rewards are many. Effective collaborations result in greater financial resources, increased human resources, an influx of new ideas, and, in many cases, new energy and increased forward motion. True full-sharing partnerships also provide a means of circumventing the bugaboo of almost all organizations—turf wars.

The partnerships formed by the nonprofits and government agencies we've studied all have the following characteristics in common:

- Partners were chosen carefully for compatibility of values, goals, and ways of working.
- Partners began working together in a small way and then built upon their successes.
- All partners are continually acknowledged as "owning the program."
- Partnerships are maintained face to face.
- Partners are never taken for granted.
- Partners are in for the long haul.

In the following pages we describe some amazing partnerships that demonstrate how the whole can truly be greater than the sum of its parts. Each of the organizations that embraces these partnerships gives us a new lesson in mathematics. For when it comes to partnerships, one plus one can equal six, or eight, or even fifty-four.

Effective Partnerships Are Built Step by Step

Our candidate for all-around champion partnership is the Medical Care for Children Project (MCCP) in Fairfax County, Virginia. This is a partnership that supplies the full range of medical and dental services to 8,000 children of the county's working poor. The MCCP provides acute care, well-child examinations, X rays, tests, immunizations, and mental health care management. Participants in the project include more than three hundred physicians and specialists, nine pharmacies, five medical laboratories, fifty-seven dentists, three oral surgeons, two major HMOs, and an urgent care center.

At the center of this web of partnerships sits Sandra Stiner Lowe, executive director of MCCP, Office of Partnerships, Department of Community Action (DCA).

With a median family income of more than $90,000 a year and the average price of a new house in excess of $250,000, Fairfax is one of the most affluent counties in the United States. Visit the shopping plaza in the town of Reston, for example, and you can buy designer fashions, lunch on champagne and caviar, and stroll through stores with names like Gucci, Marc Cross, Hermes, and Armani. But less than two miles away, children suffer because their families cannot afford the medical treatment they require. Mothers are forced to decide whether to spend their remaining funds on a pair of shoes for one child or on asthma medicine for another.

These are the working poor. The parents of these families—a large percentage are single parents—work and work hard. With family incomes between $6,000 and $15,000, they find themselves above the Medicaid and welfare assistance cutoffs and far below what is required to provide their children with medical care once the rent is paid and clothing and food are purchased.

In 1986, Sandra Lowe and her DCA staff conducted an in-depth survey of this population. To their astonishment, they discovered that more than 78,000 individuals in the county had no medical insurance and that 19,000 of these were children. "Many of these children," says Lowe, "had never seen a physician, or had seen one only in an emergency room. This was a population that was accustomed to not going to the doctor unless they were near death. The fever had to spike at 105 degrees and stay there."

The DCA survey made the problem alarmingly clear but offered no solutions. The county had limited resources, and there were no federal or state funds upon which to draw. So Sandy Lowe and her staff decided to forge a public-private partnership to bring decent medical care to these forgotten youngsters. The steps they took went to create and sustain the MCCP provide a primer on how an effective partnership can be established.

"From the beginning," says Lowe, "we all realized that in order for the project to work we would have to have the involvement of the county government, the medical community, and the business community. We knew if we worked together we could get the results we needed." Lowe and her staff began by enlisting the support of the business community. They were determined to find a business leader who would take the project to heart, head a concerted fundraising effort, and bring in other business leaders. "What is crucial," says Lowe, "is to get the participation of a person who is so well respected in the community that others will follow his or her lead." She found that person in Eric Erdossy, the president of the First American Bank of Northern Virginia. Erdossy, along with fellow banker Bob H. Hawthorne, immediately began to spearhead a drive that would not only get the project off the ground but would provide long-term financing.

At the same time that Lowe and her DCA colleague Richard Olson were establishing their ties with the business community, they were also seeking to recruit another vital partner, an HMO that could provide the widest range of medical services at the lowest cost possible. "We knew," says Lowe, "that in order for the project to work the way we wanted it to, we would have to have a major HMO involved early on. We started to get bogged down in discussions on how to accomplish this, so I just picked up the yellow pages and selected the name of the chief of pediatrics at Kaiser Permanente's Springfield facility. We went to see him armed with a profile of our children and said, 'We'd like you to begin by taking care of fifty of our kids and we have no money to pay you.' He looked at us, chuckled, and then got us a meeting with his regional director, who agreed to begin Kaiser's involvement by providing care for thirty-five of our youngsters. Just before we went to see him, one of the private physicians we had already enlisted bet us that we couldn't get an HMO involved. He said he'd provide free care for twenty children if we pulled if off. And I held him to it."

Kaiser Permanente now treats a thousand MCCP youngsters per year at its three Fairfax County facilities. Parents pay only one dollar per visit, while the MCCP reimburses Kaiser Permanente $264 per child per year. "The involvement of Kaiser Permanente," says Sandy Lowe, "has been an essential part of our success. They provide the full range of medical services to all of our children, and they treat them exactly as they do their regular patients. And they never say 'no' to us. For example, we found out that almost all the families we serve were without thermometers or the means to purchase over-the-counter medications not covered in the prescription plan. We mentioned that to the folks at Kaiser. Shortly thereafter, we were provided with digital thermometers for everyone and over-the-counter medications became a part of the pharmacy plan."

From the beginning, the MCCP's third partner has been the county government. The Department of Community Action initiated the program and the County Board of Supervisors supplied the project with its first operating funds. The county government contracts with neighborhood agencies to provide trained social workers, who identify eligible children and their families, enroll them, arrange their medical appointments, transport them to the medical facilities, and, where needed, supply translation services. Says Dr. Larry Kelly, physician-in-chief of Kaiser Permanente's operations in northern Virginia, "I cannot overstate how important the individual case workers are to this project. Don't forget, we're dealing with people who, out of necessity, have a long history of deferring medical attention. Without the case workers, the clients would not find out about the programs and would not get to the doctors."

"If you pulled any of the partners out," says Fred Nebel, head of Kaiser's community relations, "this project wouldn't exist. Since the partnership was built carefully, step by step, that is something that just won't happen." This understanding of the need to proceed incrementally and to build on small wins has been essential to the MCCP's success. The strategy was essential to Eric Erdossy's and Bob Hawthorne's fundraising efforts. "We knew," says Hawthorne, "that in a project like this, it would be important to focus first on raising initial seed money. Raising this early money allowed us to demonstrate success, which paved the way for going after much larger sums. So it was at the very beginning that we called in the chits."

Effective Partnerships Plan for the Long Term

Those who created the MCCP did so with the understanding that there would always be a need for the services it would provide. From the very beginning, their plans included exploring ways to ensure that the project would become a permanent fixture of the community. "Even as we began targeting our first potential contributors," says Eric Erdossy, "we were also making plans for the future of the project. We explored several avenues and found what we were looking for through the Northern Virginia Community Foundation. Thanks to this foundation and its director, Florence Townsend, we were able to create an endowment fund that has benefited MCCP in numerous ways. First of all, it enables donors to contribute to a tax-exempt entity outside of county government. Secondly, our association with the foundation has enabled those of us charged with raising money for the project to expand our contacts throughout the philanthropic community. Most important, the endowment guarantees the existence of the project forever."

Make Sure All Partners Own the Program

One of the MCCP's distinguishing characteristics is the way in which each of the project's partners shares the pride of ownership that accompanies the success of the program. "If you talk to the business people," says Fred Nebel, "they tell you it's their program. If you talk to the county people, they also say it's their program. And if you ask us at Kaiser Permanente, we'll tell you the same thing."

Partnerships Must Be Maintained Face to Face

The MCCP partnership is fortified by bringing all of the partners together as often as possible. Says Dr. Larry Kelly, "I think the fact that all of us involved in the project meet together regularly is key to its success. It enables us, no matter how busy we are, to keep the project in mind and to keep coming up with fresh ideas to improve, refine, and expand it. We're constantly setting goals, assessing performance, discussing the possibility of new programs. Recently we moved into medical care for adolescents, and we continually inform and involve all of the partners in order to get the level of commitment and contribution that this new endeavor requires." Says Sandy Lowe, "We see absolutely no barriers or limitations to what we can accomplish. As a government agency, we have total access to our partners. Anytime I need to talk to anyone at Kaiser Permanente or any of our private physicians, they'll really listen to me. The same is true of people like Hugh Long and Gail Graham at First Union Bank, which took over First American. They are always there when we need them."

True Partners Don't Take Each Other for Granted

"We believe," says Lowe, "that it's terribly important to always let our partners know that we're aware of their accomplishments and how much we appreciate what they're doing. And so there are a lot of small things that we do to thank them and recognize their efforts. We send out balloons that say, 'Thank you for caring.' We send out flowers or cards acknowledging a particular achievement. And we make sure that in whatever publicity we get, we mention the participation of all our partners." Says Larry Kelly, "You get these little notes or a poem or a card from Sandy thanking you for what you've just done. It's a great motivator. You're constantly reminded of the fact that the project has become an important part of your life. And we've all learned from Sandy. Here at Kaiser we now make a real effort to keep all of our people informed of what's going on in the project. They start to get some real recognition for what they're doing and the whole thing mushrooms. We'd still be proud of our contributions even if they went unnoticed, but the recognition takes it into another realm."

Partnerships Thrive if All Partners Thrive

"From a self-serving point of view," says Kaiser's Nebel, "we've gotten wonderful publicity out of being involved in MCCP. And since we've already got the facilities and the physicians, it really doesn't cost us that much in terms of our overall budget." Elizabeth Lusk, pediatric clinical coordinator at the Reston facility, points out another benefit to Kaiser. "All of us in the health care field are in competition for the best-qualified nurses. Our involvement in this project has helped us attract some excellent people, who came to us because they were interested in helping the kind of youngsters that this program serves." Says one Fairfax County case worker, "Ours can be a very tough profession. Seeing the results that we help get with these children truly helps us to carry on."

The satisfaction gained from helping youngsters in need is shared by the MCCP's business partners, who, like their collaborators in the medical profession, derive practical benefits from the project as well. "Under any circumstances it would be important to do everything we can for these youngsters," says a First Union official. "The added payoff for us comes in knowing that many of those we are helping will be our customers in the future."

Since its founding in 1986, the MCCP has created a remarkable record of achievement. To date, some 30,000 children have been served by the project, and plans are well under way for additional services that will reach out to new segments of Fairfax County's population. The most important accolades come from those the project serves. Pearl Royal is a single parent with five children ranging in age from ten to four. She is an articulate Fairfax County schoolbus driver who works as many shifts as her supervisors will allow. Says Royal, "I cannot adequately tell you what the Medical Care for Children Project means to me and my children. For example, my six-year-old daughter developed a serious rash. If we weren't in this program I'd have just put some alcohol on it and tried to make her comfortable. Being in the program, I called the advice line and spoke to a nurse, who set up an immediate appointment for me. When I brought my daughter in they took a culture and discovered that she had strep throat. Without this program, this condition would never have been treated and my daughter could have developed rheumatic fever. It saved her health and it saved me because I know I would have blamed myself for not being able to afford the help she needed. It would have just destroyed me."

In our conversations with Pearl Royal, she revealed another characteristic of the program that means so much to her. "This program takes care of my children," she says, "in a way that always preserves our dignity. I can't tell you how important that is. In the past, I've been on a food-stamp program, and there were so many times I'd do my grocery shopping and then go up to the checkout counter and the person there would be so nice until I began to pay with my stamps. Immediately her attitude would change. That just doesn't happen in this program. They care about me, they take care of my kids, they're always telling me about new ways they can help us, and they do it without ever saying anything about our financial situation."

Use Partnerships to Overcome Turf Battles

When Rose Washington was director of New York's Division of Juvenile Justice (DJJ), she was quick to point out, "You spend an inordinate amount of time surmounting obstacles, large and small. And one of the greatest barriers to getting things done involves battles over turf."

It is an ancient issue faced by every organization, public or private. The DJJ, like several other organizations we studied, has found that through working partnerships issues of turf can be most successfully combated. "In establishing one of our programs," explains Washington, "we ran into real problems because people in the city's probation department felt that they weren't involved enough and that we were stepping into areas that they perceived as being within their domain. It got real hairy and it was getting in the way of the program." The DJJ met the issue head on by forming a working partnership with the probation department and bringing them fully into the process of developing the program. "We didn't just give it lip service or try to make them partners in name only," says veteran DJJ legal counsel Kay Murray. "We made it clear from the beginning that this was to be a full collaboration with both partners fully involved."

Probation department partners attended every meeting held during the development of the program. Each of their suggestions was carefully considered, and each of their contributions was publicly recognized. Says Murray, "In any organizational endeavor, issues over turf will always be present. It's simply human nature. I don't know of any better way to overcome this issue than by creating partnerships in which everyone has a vested interest, everyone feels their contributions are important, and everyone shares in the challenges and the rewards."

Awareness of the need to overcome turf issues has, in large measure, led to the success achieved in Pennsylvania by Northumberland County's Children's Clinic. The agency serves its clients and their families by bringing together, on an equal footing, staff members from every department of the county's human services department. Line workers within the various departments are given full decision-making power and the authority to commit departmental resources. "Bringing everyone together and giving them real power and a real vested interest," says former county counseling service head Ellen Wolf, "is what keeps things functioning and growing. It's what eliminates struggles over whose job it is, and that leads to quality service."

True Partners are In for the Long Haul

For many years, visitors to The Nature Conservancy's Arlington, Virginia, headquarters were greeted by a scoreboard that hung high on a wall behind the receptionist's desk. In the 1990s, the numbers on the scoreboard changed so rapidly that the board deteriorated. If it had still been up in January 1997, the figures would have read as follows: ACRES SAVED IN THE UNITED STATES—9.3 MILLION; ACRES PROTECTED OUTSIDE THE UNITED STATES—57 MILLION; ACRES MANAGED— 1.5 million. To date, TNC has completed more land deals than real-estate giant Coldwell Banker. But this organization is not in business just to make deals. It's purpose is to save endangered plants and animals.

Since 1953, TNC has established more than 1,500 natural preserves, forming the largest nongovernmental sanctuary system in the world. In addition, it has handed over millions of acres to local, state, and federal agencies. Along the way, it has purchased or been given millions of acres of land that host no endangered species and then has sold this land and used the proceeds to purchase parcels where endangered species do live.

In order to protect endangered plants and animals, TNC has created and maintained the most complete biological database in the world. Within each of the fifty U.S. states, TNC botanists, zoologists, and ecologists monitor all of the state's plants and animals based on existing records and their own continual observations. They file and record the names and locations of endangered species on computer, ranking each according to the degree to which it is endangered. Taken together, these surveys make up TNC's Natural Heritage Program.

One of the key ingredients in the TNC success story is the way in which the organization undertakes collaborative efforts with outside groups. The Natural Heritage Program, for example, is based on partnerships with appropriate state government agencies. "For us," explains the program's head, Mark Shaffer, "it's a genuine, thoroughgoing integration. In each of the states, we've found someone in state government sufficiently interested in the program to get started. Of the fifty state programs, forty are now more or less fully transferred into state control. Our job here at the Conservancy is to train all of the staff and to maintain the technical part of the operation, including the central databases. But we're very careful not to upstage our partners."

The Natural Heritage Program operates not only in the fifty states but in Canada and Latin America as well. In Latin America the

Conservancy has established conservation data centers in eighteen participating countries. There TNC works in partnership with government and nonprofits to preserve land containing endangered plants and animals. It also assists these nations in identifying and preserving huge areas that TNC has labeled Parks in Peril. The ambitious goal of the Parks in Peril program is to protect two hundred key sites containing more than 100 million acres by the year 2000.

Since it is almost impossible for foreigners to acquire lands for conservation purposes in Latin America, the TNC supports nongovernmental partner organizations within various participating countries. Conservancy support includes the development of innovative ways to raise the money needed for conservation. For example, the TNC has pioneered a "debt-for-nature" swap in various Latin American countries. In Costa Rica, for instance, the TNC bought almost $6 million of discounted Costa Rican debt for about $750,000 from the American Express Bank. The Conservancy then converted the debt to Costa Rican currency bonds valued at $1.7 million. In five years, the bonds generated more than $3 million in interest. The TNC then turned over that money to Costa Rica for the purpose of training conservationists, protecting wildlife parks, and acquiring land for preserves. The Conservancy is now pursuing similar arrangements in Ecuador, Peru, Brazil, Guatemala, and Jamaica.

"Partnership," says the TNC's former Latin American director Geoff Barnard, "is key to everything that the Conservancy has accomplished overseas. It focuses on providing guidance on fundraising, on training, on inventorying with its in-country partners. And it believes in continuity almost as much as it believes in sticking to its mission. When TNC starts working with a partner in Brazil or Argentina or Peru, they know the Conservancy is in for the long haul. This is a much different approach than that used by other conservation organizations who obtain grants and then regrant them. TNC has worked hard to get out of the grant-making business. Although it does move a lot of money and resources to its partners, it does so in a unique, collaborative way. It listens to their needs, works toward setting a common agenda, and then helps them meet it."

Barnard has a favorite anecdote that he uses to stress the effectiveness of the Conservancy's partnership approach: "When I was TNC's Latin American director, I was invited to a strategic planning session in Peru," he recalls, "and I suggested that representatives from another group that had given them a substantial amount of money be at the meeting. When I arrived, no one from that organization was there. After the meeting I asked why this was so. The Peruvians replied by saying, 'Oh, they're just a donor; you're our partner.' That is exactly what TNC has always been about. When those they are trying to serve truly see them as partners in their endeavors, then they're not afraid to reveal their weaknesses, their strengths and their problems. And that's when things get done."

Maximize Your Partnership by Placing Power as Close to the Action as You Can

Historically, partnerships involving federal, state, and local agencies have been characterized by a collaboration in which the federal agencies set the standards and sign the checks and federal and state agencies carry out the programs. The most effective partnerships are structured in a much different way. The award-winning Striving Toward Excellence in Performance (STEP) program in Minnesota created dozens of model partnerships. For instance, the Minnesota Department of Transportation created an alliance of public and private partners to develop the first automated weather station network. The same department developed a program to train air traffic controllers better and more cheaply than the Federal Aviation Administration (FAA) could, then sold the FAA a training partnership.

One of the most effective government partnerships we encountered involved the Water Resources Division of the U.S. Geological Survey (USGS). The USGS has been in business for almost 120 years. It has had only twelve directors in that entire span, a continuity of leadership unique in federal government. "We have to be good," says the survey's public affairs officer, Don Kelly. "We have the ghosts of giants breathing down our necks."

A bureau of the Department of the Interior, the USGS was established to follow the example of Lewis and Clark in surveying the vast wilderness areas of the American West. Many people still identify the agency with the detailed topographical maps it publishes, and the folks at the USGS are justifiably proud of these, but the agency does a whole lot more. Today the survey undertakes an extraordinary range of tasks, all in keeping with its motto, "earth science in the public service." Says survey geologist Ben Morgan, "Many of the major issues that became emblazoned in the public consciousness in the 1970s and 1980s—water and air pollution, coastal erosion, the threatened ozone layer, global warming—these are all earth science issues. And they've been brought into the public arena. For the survey and its mission, they've brought great opportunity and great responsibility as well."

The USGS is organized into four major program divisions—geologic, national mapping, water resources, and biological resources. The geologic division, with a staff of about 2,800, provides information on land resources, energy, and mineral resources, and geologic hazards of the nation and its territories. The water resources division employs about 4,700 people and provides information on the quantity and quality of the nation's surface water resources. The national mapping division, through its approximately 1,800 employees, provides maps and technical assistance and conducts related research responsive to national needs. And the biological resources division, with its 1,700 employees, represents a recent addition to the scope and responsibilities of the USGS. In 1996, the U.S. Congress directed the survey to absorb the former National Biological Service. Through its new biological resources division, the survey now carries out the biological research that was formerly conducted by several separate agencies of the Department of the Interior, including the Fish and Wildlife Service, the Bureau of Land Management, and the National Park Service.

Because each of the divisions has its own objectives and performs its own distinct tasks, each is managed differently. The national mapping division, one of the few government entities that produces and sells products, is run much like a private corporation, complete with product managers, marketing experts, sales personnel, and the like. The geologic division, aware of the importance of involving its scientists directly in decisions that affect their fieldwork, brings these scientists in from the field on a rotating basis to serve in managerial capacities in the survey's national headquarters in Reston, Virginia. The water resources division, which by 1997 had grown to 4,800 employees, nearly half the USGS's total workforce, is run on a highly decentralized basis, with its partnership with state and local agencies at the heart of its operations. The biological resources division is so relatively new that a particular management style has not been put into place. Typical of the way USGS operates, several management approaches will be tried in order to determine which is most effective for this particular division.

Chief hydrologist and chief of the water resources division Dr. Robert Hirsch is quick to point out that "We are totally characterized by the ways in which we operate in full partnership with over 1,200 state and local agencies." Dr. Hirsch's division maintains over 40,000 gauging stations around the country, each of which checks the availability and chemistry of water in a certain area. The information the division gathers from these thousands of stations is transmitted to a satellite and then relayed to the survey's general data bank. The information is then made available to the water division's state, local, and federal agency partners. Most of the stream flow data that the National Weather Service and the local weather forecasting organizations use to forecast floods comes from the data gathered at these gauging stations. The water resources division, through its partnership with the Department of Defense, also provides vital services to the U.S. Army Corps of Engineers. "You build dams and bridges based on the availability of water supply," says

Dr. Hirsch, "and you build highway crossings and other parts of the national infrastructure based on hydrologic statistics. That's all based on the data this one division and its partners gather and disseminate."

One of the survey's state partners is the South Florida Water Management District. Says its director, Dr. Leslie Wedderburn, "Our relationship with the survey is a partnership in the fullest sense of the word. Neither this agency nor the survey could accomplish what needs to be done alone. The survey provides us a national perspective on hydrological issues that we just would not have without its input. USGS also provides us with technical assistance that is vital to our work. For example, through the survey's sophisticated satellite network we receive critical information on impending floods and storm surges. The survey constantly monitors national trends in all areas dealing with the quantity and quality of water and immediately passes on to us any information pertaining to our region.

"We contribute to the partnership in several ways," continues Wedderburn. "First of all, we contribute funds from our state budget. The task of collecting all the data related to this nation's surface water resources could never be adequately carried out solely on the money that the survey receives from the United States Congress. Just as important, we are totally responsible for gathering every type of hydrological data for our region and feeding the information to the survey. The survey understands that we're best qualified to do this since we have a more detailed involvement with local officials and with local issues. The decision-making authority that USGS gives us in dealing with local data gathering and other issues is what makes this partnership so successful."

Peter G. Morros is the director of the Department of Conservation and Natural Resources for the state of Nevada. "The survey," he says, "holds regular conferences to which we're all invited, where experts from every area concerned with hydrological matters not only introduce us to the latest technology and trends but listen to our specific problems and give us valued advice. The main reason, however, that the partnership works so effectively is that the USGS treats all of us at the state and local levels as equals with those at the survey. USGS officials constantly visit with us at our sites, asking what they can contribute to making our data-gathering more efficient. Most important, they listen carefully and respond to what we feel needs to be done. It is this respect for our knowledge and our work that is the key to all that this partnership accomplishes."

From its inception, the Centers for Disease Control and Prevention (CDC) has worked hand in hand with state and local partners. Just as local constables in Great Britain call on Scotland Yard for help in major cases, local agencies throughout America call in the CDC to investigate health problems that baffle or overwhelm them. The CDC exchanges vital statistics with local agencies and helps devise and support local prevention efforts. The agency's effectiveness within these partnerships is enhanced by the fact that many CDC staff, including former director Dr. William Roper, have worked at the state and local level, and many local health officials have served a stint at the CDC.

Roper, who served as CDC director until 1993, committed the institution to intensifying these partnerships. "I knew that there was much more that we could do," he says, "and that we ought to be doing, to help strengthen the network for protecting the public's health in this country." According to Roper, the key ingredient in the nation's public health infrastructure is not the CDC but the local public health agency. Much of the director's efforts were put toward channeling the CDC's resources into assessing and strengthening local city, state, and county agencies, which range from those with giant research departments to one-nurse operations in small towns. "Local health departments should assume the community leadership role," says Roper. "They should set forth the health agenda, build the necessary networks and alliances, mobilize support, and put together public and private resources for common health purposes. This," he states, "is a bottom-up process, which means that sometimes their priorities might not be what the CDC director would pick or even what the state health department might pick, but for this partnership to be effective the real power has to be placed where the action is, and that's at the local level."

Effective Partnerships Make Innovative Programs Possible

In their determination to help meet the challenges faced by girls from all walks of life, the Girl Scouts of the U.S. (GSUSA) identified a segment of the population that was in particular need—young girls whose mothers were incarcerated. In order to provide a meaningful program for these youngsters by tapping into needed experience, expertise, and facilities, the Central Maryland Girl Scout Council, in 1992, formed a partnership with the National Institute of Justice and created the Girl Scouts Beyond Bars program. Along with providing activities, education, and counseling for the girls, the program also provides parent education workshops for the incarcerated mothers and continues to work with the girls and their moms once the mothers are released from prison. In 1996, Girl Scouts Beyond Bars was expanded from fifteen to twenty-five Girl Scout councils. The program, from the beginning, has been so successful that today it is supported at sites throughout the country with funds from private donations, foundations, and state agencies. A 1997 list of the Girl Scouts' partners in this important endeavor reveals the diversity of partners a public-service organization can tap to bring needed human and financial resources to a project:

Maryland
Maryland Division of
Corrections
United Way of Central
Maryland
Private Donations

Arizona
Arizona Community
Foundation
Arizona Governor's Office for
Children
Valley of the Sun
United Way
Thunderbird Youth Fund

Tallahassee, Florida
Community Juvenile Justice
Partnership Program
(Administered by the
Florida Attorney General's
Office)

New Jersey
Schumann Fund of New Jersey
Prudential Foundation

Fort Lauderdale, Florida
Henderson Foundation
Mount Bethel Baptist Church
Florida Department of Mental
Health Services

Kentucky
Anonymous Gift
City of Louisville Youth Alliance
Mercer Transportation Company

Delaware
DuPont Merck
Pharmaceutical Company

California
The Edison Company

Use Partnerships to Reduce Duplication of Services

"There are many benefits to partnerships," says the U.S. Forest Service's Rod Collins, "and in government agencies, one of the greatest is the opportunity that collaborations present for eliminating the duplication of services." Collins is the coordinator of a partnership between the Ochoco National Forest, the Department of the Interior's Bureau of Land Management, and the Deschutes National Forest.

"Too many times in government," says Collins, "we find two or more agencies offering the same services to basically the same customers. The purpose of this partnership is to explore every way possible in which we can combine resources to eliminate this costly and needless exercise."

Every Friday, management and employees from the three partner agencies gather for their Oregon Chowder Lunch, at which they discuss issues and assign leadership teams, made up of individuals from all three organizations, to act upon those targeted for action. "In our determination to eliminate duplication and to better serve our customers in general," says Collins, "we focus on areas

where there is a high probability of success on an issue so significant to the public that it cries out to be addressed."

This simple yet effective partnership has already achieved some
significant results, including the following:

- Four separate fire-fighting dispatch centers have been combined into one efficient interagency fire dispatch center for
  central Oregon. This unified team has responsibility for
  more acres than any other fire dispatch center in the nation.
- Range administration and management of recreational resources are now shared by the three agencies.
- Instead of each agency producing its own map of the area,
  the partnership has produced one more complete and more
  user friendly map of the region.

True Partners Help Set the Standards

In its efforts to bring about systemwide reform, the Rochester, New
York, school district has learned that the enthusiastic commitment
of the business community is essential to the goals it is striving to
achieve. More than three hundred partnerships involving more than
twenty Rochester-area businesses are now in place, providing a
variety of vital services. One of the keys in making this happen
initially was the School and Business Alliance (SABA), a statewide
initiative for helping the business community understand how,
through public-private partnerships, a school district could dramatically improve its fortunes. "In any community," says Peggy Weston
Byrd, who was SABA's project administrator, "there are business
leaders who want to get involved in helping the schools. The problem is that people don't know how to approach the schools or what
specifically they can do to help. What they need to be told is that
what you can do is limited only by your imagination. You can loan
your executives to the schools to help bring about systemic change;
you can get your people involved in bringing to the schools their
expertise in marketing, accounting, and engineering. You can use
your people to help the schools bring the real world to the classroom. And you can provide job opportunities, training, and incentives for youngsters while they're in school and after they
graduate."

SABA provided a key link between Rochester's schools and its
businesses, and the business community responded positively.
Executives from Xerox and Kodak, Rochester's biggest employers,
have loaned executives to the school district to help train teachers
and administrators and to aid in strategic planning and in implementing the district's school-to-work program. Both of these cor-

porations, along with other Rochester businesses, have sponsored a host of tutorial programs, science and math clubs, literacy programs, library programs, work-study projects, career programs, and competitions in every academic area.

The executives on loan from Xerox and Kodak had an enormous impact on Rochester's systemwide reform efforts. Along with other contributions, they helped the superintendent and school leadership implement a strategic plan based on specific benchmarks for program performance, including target numbers. Beginning in the 1995–96 school year, their goal was to increase by 25 percent a year the number of students in FICA-paying jobs and the number of students in work-based learning experiences. In addition, they aimed to increase the number of youth apprenticeships for high school students by at least 50 percent each year, with a goal of 300 apprenticeships by 1999.

Thanks to the help of the Rochester business community, these benchmarks were not only met but exceeded. In July 1996, 679 Rochester students participated in work-based learning experiences, a 31 percent increase over the previous year. In addition, 58 students were in youth apprenticeships, an increase of 53 percent.

Rochester's passionate commitment to school-business partnerships has also been aided by a $1 million grant that it received from the federal government for its prekindergarten through adult education school-to-work transition program. The school district has also benefited from an organization formed in 1996 called the Rochester Business Alliance (RBA). Made up of twenty-two large Rochester businesses, including Gannett, Bausch and Lomb, and Xerox, the alliance hopes to gain an important return on investment for its member companies by supporting programs that feature work-based learning opportunities.

True Partners Must Go the Extra Mile

One of the most acclaimed partnerships within the Rochester district is the one sponsored by the Wegmans Food and Pharmacy chain. Under this partnership, Wegmans provides part-time jobs in its supermarkets for fourteen- and fifteen-year-old students who may need special motivation to complete their high school educations. Wegmans not only provides the jobs but also supplies weekend transportation to and from work. Most important, it sponsors preemployment and follow-up workshops to help students understand the relationship between school and work and provides each student with an on-the-job mentor who guides and supports the student-employee. Wegmans also arranges tutoring for each student-employee who needs help with his or her schoolwork. To every student who adheres to the guidelines of the program and successfully completes a high school education, the company provides the same tuition benefits it gives to its full-time employees—50 percent of tuition up to $1,500 a year to enroll at any accredited institution of his or her choice. Students also are given the opportunity to keep their jobs with Wegmans.

The Wegmans program has been so successful that it has been significantly expanded to include other Rochester corporations. Wegmans has introduced the program into Syracuse and Buffalo, where the food chain also has a large presence. The program, now called the Hillside Work Scholarship Connection, receives foundation and corporate grants to further its work.

True Partners

The most effective partnerships between the business community and the schools have been those in which both parties have understood that business's involvement should go beyond simply adopting schools or funding scholarships. Here are some examples of innovative and successful business involvement:

- The Whitman Company of Chicago awards $5,000 annually to twenty area principals deemed outstanding managers.
- Wells Fargo and Co. has put $200,000 into local schools, supporting efforts to increase parental responsibility and school accountability.
- The ICT Financial Corporation, in partnership with Henry High School in Minneapolis, has developed ten projects, including Power English, a literacy program required of all ninth graders that rewards top students with a savings account and money to put in it.
- Sears Roebuck sponsors an Academic Olympics in communities around the country that recognizes and rewards the achievements of average students.
- The NCNB Corporation of Charlotte, North Carolina, has donated $1 million to the Southern Regional Education Board to establish a leadership academy for teachers, principals, and school board members. A second $1 million has been set aside as prize money for schools that set performance goals and achieve them.
- IBM has committed some $60 million to a faculty loan program, which assigns IBM managers to serve as full-time teachers or school administrators.
- The Connecticut Mutual Life Insurance Company, with the full involvement of teachers, students, and school administrators, donates and administers a special fund to pay for programs that the Hartford public schools cannot otherwise afford to maintain.

◆▶

True Partners (continued)

- The Boeing Corporation assigns company representatives, called education managers, to local schools and districts where the company has operations. The managers put together partnerships for the schools. Boeing also invites teachers to participate in company management classes.
- American Express has established a career-oriented Academy of Finance in a Brooklyn, New York, high school whose success has inspired several other corporations to sponsor a total of thirty-five similar academies nationwide.

Making a Partnership Work

Sandra Stiner Lowe, architect of Fairfax County's Medical Care for Children Project, supplies the following tips for forming a successful partnership:

- At the very beginning of a partnership, make sure that all those involved are in agreement as to what the role and responsibilities of each of the partners is expected to be.
- Understand that the best partners are those willing to make long-term commitments to the project.
- Keep in constant contact with all of your partners. Keep them informed of progress made and any challenges that have arisen. Avoid surprises. If changes are needed, inform your partners as soon as possible.
- Recognize as quickly and as publicly as you can all contributions made by a partner.
- Focus on creating win/win situations with your partners. The more they win, the more they will contribute.
- Avoid issues of turf by having all partners involved in major decisions.
- Put day-to-day decision-making power in the hands of those closest to the action.

As we've seen, the most effective partnerships are those in which new ideas are continually brought to the collaboration. All organizations need new ideas, whether they are involved in partnerships or not. Put simply, no organization can succeed by standing still. The constant flow of new ideas motivates staff, combats complacency, allows for dramatic turnarounds, and keeps the best organizations on top of their game, all of which we'll discover in the next chapter on innovation.

7

CREATING A
CLIMATE FOR
INNOVATION

Every organization profiled in this book makes a habit of innovation. Each believes that it must continually improve itself and find new ways of doing things or fall by the wayside.

What is innovation? What makes an organization innovative? Here's what we noticed in our visits to innovative organizations:

The signs of innovation are everywhere. Innovative organizations engage their employees in improving everything. Innovation flourishes as people meet and talk, formally and informally. When face-to-face meetings aren't possible, these organizations invest in technologies that allow people to share ideas and problems with colleagues around the country.

A spirit of restlessness prevails. Innovative organizations are never satisfied. They're not smug about being *the* museum in town or *the* agency that has won the latest performance award. People in innovative organizations are both intellectually and physically restless. Physically, employees don't linger at their desks. They are up and moving, talking to coworkers, building collaborations, getting the job done and suggesting new ways to do it. Intellectually, these same folks are brazenly curious. During our many visits, we were crossexamined about our own project and queried about all the organizations we were visiting. When our interviewees heard about a strategy they felt they could use, they asked for a name and phone number so they could check it out.

Problem solving is high on the agenda. Most of the organizations we studied have no surplus resources with which to tackle problems. Yet they are characterized by the way in which they face up to inevitable problems and concentrate on finding solutions. When we sat in on problem-solving discussions, the most common

115

questions we heard were: "What needs to be done?" "How soon?" and "Who can help?"

Optimism is the rule.   Innovative organizations cultivate and cherish people who have a "can-do" attitude. They are character- ized by a penchant for action, not reaction, and the belief that, within reason, everything is possible. Nowhere is the emphasis on problem solving more obvious than in times of cutbacks and down- sizing. Innovative organizations like the city of Phoenix turn their attention to the problem of doing more with less and consequently fare better even in bad times.

Perseverance is a way of life.   Effective organizations never stop innovating. When they are faltering, they innovate to turn their fortunes around. When they are doing well, they innovate to keep on top.

In this chapter, you will encounter the specific strategies our vanguard organizations employ to make innovation their hallmark.

All Employees Are Innovators

When Sandra J. Hale became Minnesota's commissioner of admin- istration in 1983, she inherited a troubled agency. State employees were fond of saying that DOA stood not for Department of Adminis- tration but for "dead on arrival." Over the next eight years, Hale changed the way her agency did business and, in the process, turned it into an agent of change for the entire state government.

In her second year on the job, Hale brought together a group of state managers, corporate executives, and academics to model a program to foster long-term change in government, one that would improve productivity and efficiency by capitalizing on people's strengths. The panel came up with a set of six hypotheses that became the foundation of a program they named STEP (Striving toward Excellence in Performance), a service-oriented, bottom-up program of innovation based on these premises:

- Closer contact and interaction with customers provide a better understanding of the customers' needs.
- Increased employee participation taps the knowledge, skills, and commitment of all state workers.
- Increased discretion gives managers and employees greater control over and accountability for a bottom line.
- Partnerships allow the sharing of knowledge, expertise, and other resources.
- State-of-the-art techniques enhance productivity.
- Improved work measurement provides a base for planning and implementing service improvements and giving work- ers information about their performance.

With a board of top executives from all sectors, STEP put out a call to state employees, asking them to propose ideas for improvement along with specific goals or outcomes that would help achieve them. Employees were asked also to identify potential allies who could help bring about the innovation. If the improvement idea incorporated the six STEP principles, it went to the STEP steering committee, which reviewed the project. The project might be approved and sent back to the suggester with ideas for strengthening, or it might be bounced back as not being within STEP's purview. If the project was accepted, STEP provided the team with training in creative problem solving, work measurement, employee involvement, and productivity improvement techniques and worked to create opportunities for partnerships with other public- and private-sector organizations. No new resources were assigned to STEP projects, and participants were not given time off to work on their STEP programs.

Despite the constraints, response to STEP was enthusiastic and results were astounding. One of the first successful STEP projects involved the state parks department, which is called the Department of Natural Resources (DNR). One-third of the department's budget came from park entrance fees, but attendance was dropping, so department managers developed strategies to market the park. The DNR surveyed visitors and introduced new services. By accepting credit card payments and forging a partnership with a private gift shop concern, it boosted revenues. As one DNR employee puts it, "We started thinking that the people, not the trees, were our customers."

John McLagan of the Department of Corrections was the manager of another STEP project called Sentencing to Service, which operated in partnership with the DNR. Under this project, first-time offenders, rather than being jailed, were sentenced to serve in the state parks, cleaning up forest fire debris, repairing drainage ditches, thinning timber. The program resulted in a significant two-to-one cost savings to taxpayers, reducing the need for new prison beds. One county saved $32,000 in just six months. Says McLagan, "I've never had anyone shake my hand for locking him up in jail, but they shook my hand over this." And McLagan points to the fact that some offenders, in order to finish a job, actually volunteered to stay on with a work crew a day or two after their sentences were completed.

Perhaps the best endorsement for STEP was the way it developed participants. Dean Larson of the Department of Transportation is a case in point. Larson, a STEP manager, and his team brought in thirty-three public and private partners to develop the nation's first automated weather station network. He built a tornado warning system for local sheriffs and found donations to cover the costs.

Larson also created a partnership with the Federal Aviation Administration (FAA), under the terms of which his agency trained air-traffic controllers less expensively and more successfully than the FAA could itself. The dropout rate at Minnesota's air-traffic control training school was 7 percent, compared with 40 percent at the federally run program.

Making Change Happen

Following are precepts that the staff of Minnesota's STEP program identified as fundamental for creating innovation or change:

- Employee ownership of the change is a must.
- Change must be visibly promoted by top management.
- Change must have visible and effective results.
- Change takes a long time.
- Mistakes must be considered opportunities for corrective action or refinement.
- Training and technical assistance must be provided.
- The change process must be managed.
- Any change must have a clearly stated, realistic goal.

Having listed these precepts, the folks at STEP then identified the following specific stages for making innovation a reality:

- Determine and create an awareness of the need for change. For any long-term change to succeed, it must first identify its primary audience.
- Assess the work environment before designing the change.
- Design the program. What are the constraints? What criteria will be used to evaluate the design? How will the final design decision be made? Who will be involved? How will design decisions be communicated?
- Assess the impact. Consider mission/strategy, culture/values, leadership style, management process, products/services, and policy and procedures.
- Organize for change.
- Maintain the momentum.
- Celebrate the change.
- Evaluate the change process.
- Fine-tune the process.

Overcome Bureaucracy through Innovation

One of the biggest turnarounds accomplished by STEP took place in the state motor pool. When Hale assumed her position, state employees would do anything to avoid using the dirty and unreliable state cars. The manager of the central motor pool was aware of customer complaints and realized that he should run his business like Avis. But in practice, bureaucratic traditions were stronger than any customer service imperative. On his own initiative, the manager began to take actions to turn the motor pool around. When, for example, a car was returned to the pool full of debris, he cleaned the car, boxed the debris, and mailed it to the person who had messed up the car.

Thanks to STEP, sweeping changes took place throughout the motor pool. Bob McNeil, who headed the department, began to refer to his operation as "Hervis" because, like Hertz, it was #1, and, like Avis, it tried harder. He ran a clean, customer-focused business that competed on the open market for customers. And state employees got a bonus when they "hired" McNeil. He became their spokesman with the public. His favorite job was to field that citizen question common to all states and cities: "Was that state car I just saw really being used for official business?" McNeil took such questions, checked the records, and called the questioner back. When someone asked, "What's a state car doing putting a boat in the water on Sunday?" he could honestly reply, "That was an employee of the Department of Natural Resources stocking fish." Or when a citizen asked, "What was that person doing coming out of a deli carrying his laundry and getting in a state car at 2 o'clock last Wednesday?" he could say, "That was a health inspector, and he's required to wear that white coat during inspections."

Don't Let Rules and Regulations Stand in Your Way

As successful as it was, STEP was only the first part of the Minnesota Department of Administration's success story. Even while STEP projects were encouraging new ways of doing business in every corner of state government, Hale and her team were upgrading their own operations with a program they called Enterprise Management, which represented a fundamental change from the emphasis on control and regulation that characterized years gone by. They took a hard look at the operations of the Department of Administration and proposed the following goals:

- Separation of service and control.
- Introduction of marketplace dynamics.
- Winning compliance through leadership.
- Replacement of control with accountability.
- Emphasis on building public-private partnerships.

The enterprise model led to a dramatic increase in efficiency throughout the agency. To illustrate the benefits of separating service from control, Deputy Commissioner Jeff Zlonis points to the purchasing department. "In 1984," says Zlonis, "in order to spend $3,000, one had to go through seven layers of bureaucracy. Spending as little as $50 required purchasing department approval. If an employee needed something that cost $3,000, his office would contact a buyer's aide, who would assess needs, contact suppliers, make a deal, write a report, and kick it up to the buyer, who would kick it up another level to someone called a buyer three, who would kick it up to the deputy director of procurement, who still couldn't approve the purchase and had to kick it up to the director of purchasing, who could approve the purchase. In the whole chain only the buyer's aide had anything to contribute to the discussion."

Under the old system it took nine months to buy a piece of furniture. Thanks to the willingness of the purchasing department's employees to change, the Enterprise Management Program reduced this process to only sixteen days by eliminating all but two bureaucratic layers in the purchasing process: purchasing agent and manager. "Essentially," says Zlonis, "the department was the victim of its own problems and was probably just striking back by inflicting them on everyone else. Physically, the department was a government-issue nightmare, with a burnt-orange rug and thirty-year-old furniture arrayed in tiny cubicles, divvied up by rank and seniority. The senior managers had solid-walled offices which monopolized all the window space. When the hierarchy changed, the walls came down and people started treating each other as professionals with something to offer rather than as widgets locked in a bureaucratic system."

Recognize and Support Front Line Innovators

The magic of STEP was that it placed the power to change in the hands of those most motivated to make the change. The project had no resources and no bureaucratic power; it just offered recognition and support to people who were ready to change. In fact, STEP as an entity was almost invisible. It had only a few formal staff members from the Department of Administration, supported by a few more borrowed from other departments to provide training and support to STEP managers. The program's executive director, Terry Bock, added STEP responsibilities to an already full plate. Members of the STEP steering committee volunteered their time to review projects. Project managers didn't get special STEP time, they simply added the project to their existing job descriptions. What STEP provided was top-level recognition, which in turn gave STEP project managers room to maneuver and credibility with their bosses and their bosses' bosses. Says Peter Benner, executive director of Council 6 of the American Federation of State, County, and Municipal Employees (AFSCME), which bargains for about 60 percent of the state's 43,000 employees, "STEP was a brilliant political cover for folks who want to bring about change." June Seery was a STEP project manager who worked on a project to get compatible personal computers for her office. Before getting involved with STEP, she says, she would never have made such a suggestion because she was seen as just a "dumb secretary." But thanks to STEP, says Seery, "I came to realize I have good ideas. The big thing STEP had going for it was that it operated out of the philosophy that everyone has wisdom."

Every Organization Benefits from an Innovative Spirit

At McKean, the federal correctional institution in Bradford, Pennsylvania, former warden Dennis Luther expected innovation from everyone, staff and inmates alike. By rewarding innovation and by responding to improvement suggestions immediately, either with action or honest feedback, Luther was able to create a constant stream of improvement.

Many of the new ideas generated at the prison came from task forces that Luther initiated. He frequently assigned people to groups charged with investigating and improving problem areas. One such task force, for instance, spearheaded an aggressive prison recycling program, which saved the prison—and taxpayers—some $60,000 a year.

Luther also created a line advisory team, a rotating group that met to share complaints, rumors, and suggestions for improvement. Under Luther's leadership, McKean's department heads met every two weeks. At these meetings, each of the twenty heads came prepared with one idea for improvement. All the ideas were reviewed, and as many as possible were approved on the spot. The management team selected the best idea and gave the person suggesting it a gold star. At the team meeting we attended, seventeen of twenty ideas were approved.

Under Luther's leadership, McKean was characterized by an atmosphere of innovation and entrepreneurship that allowed inmates to improve their own quality of life—without cost to taxpayers—and to contribute to the community surrounding McKean. The primary source of innovation was the Inmate Benefit Fund (IBF), an inmate-created and inmate-run umbrella organization. The main purpose of the IBF was to raise money to sponsor cultural and leisure activities and special programs. For example, the IBF conducted an ongoing photographic project that allowed inmates, for the reasonable price of $2.50, to have pictures taken with their visitors. The IBF owned the camera, did the developing, and made a profit on every roll of film. And the IBF benefited the community as well: Through various fundraising activities, it raised more than $20,000 for local charities.

Starting Small is Often the Best Policy

McKean's partnership program with the Bradford Ranger District of the Allegheny National Forest, which started in 1989, is a lesson in the wisdom of starting small and staying small. Twenty-six inmates from McKean's camp, a minimum-security facility within the prison, work in the forest in four teams under Forest Service crew leaders. So far, they've contributed some $2.5 million in labor, which has allowed the forest to mark trails, reforest, and accomplish other tasks not covered by their operating budget. The forest puts up plaques commemorating projects accomplished by inmates.

At the start, both the prison and forest headquarters were consulted. But Warden Dennis Luther and his counterpart at Bradford realized that involving two large Washington bureaucracies would get in the way. Instead, the two outlined their agreement in a simple five-page letter. There was no other paperwork. Under the arrangement, the Forest Service transports the crews to and from work sites and supervises them with crew chiefs who are trained at the prison. The prison supplies the workers (all volunteers until recently) and provides them with lunch and nominal pay. It is a modest operation, but it provides an effective reminder of how "keeping it simple" is often the best policy.

Institutionalize Innovation

The Girl Scouts of the U.S.A. has institutionalized innovation through its various national innovation centers—and reaped substantial benefits in the process. Under this program, a center that focused on the needs of girls in a specific region of the nation was put in place. After it had piloted new programs and met its goals, it was shut down so that the programs could be replicated in other areas of the country.

Innovation centers, for example, were established in southern California, Texas, and Appalachia. Among other new programs, the center in southern California initiated projects for developing self-esteem through teen sports and, in collaboration with Head Start, brought Daisy Scouting to Head Start graduates.

The National Center for Innovation in Appalachia, which covered seven Girl Scout councils in four states, focused its attention on creating programs designed to meet the needs of young girls in isolated Appalachian communities. In its efforts to reach these girls, the Appalachian center employed the latest technology. After discovering that many families in the region had satellite dishes and VCRs, it created a taped New Leader Training Program aimed at more than five hundred new Girl Scout leaders. "It is an important innovation," says Richard R. Roberts, who was director of the Appalachian center, "for it enables us to train leaders in mountain areas we couldn't get to when they are blocked in by snow. These leaders can then form Girl Scout troops in areas where scouting has never before been available."

The National Center for Innovation in Appalachia created partnerships with principals of schools throughout the region. Using the schools' computers, girls in newly formed troops exchanged messages and ideas, played games, and worked on scouting programs together. In addition, the Appalachian center established "breakfast clubs" in many schools in the region to involve girls in scouting before the school day began. Teachers and volunteers served as leaders for younger members of the "breakfast clubs."

Although the Appalachian center was closed according to plan, many of its programs remain active. And, typical of the way the Girl Scouts operate, when the center closed officials from both it and national headquarters were brought together to consider what lessons had been learned in running the innovation centers and how they could be applied by other Girl Scout councils around the country. The GSUSA discovered that in order for any of the models to be replicated, it was first necessary to develop relationships with the resources of the community in which the innovation was to be implemented. This has been done successfully in rural communities in some nine states, including Utah and Alaska.

At the national level, GSUSA continually restructures its mechanisms for remaining at the top of the innovation curve. In 1995, national support service teams were put into place to consult with and provide training for those involved in creating innovative programs. National headquarters also established a quality recognition team to identify and share innovative practices that have been put into place by Girl Scout councils throughout the nation.

Nothing Is Sacred Where Innovation Is Concerned

When we think of the Girl Scouts, we think almost automatically of cookies. Cookie sales have been the backbone of local troops' fundraising efforts. In 1996, for example, nearly 174,356,561 boxes of cookies were sold by girls across the nation. But the GSUSA isn't afraid to look a gift horse in the mouth. At a time when nonprofits around the country are scrambling to come up with revenue-generating ventures, the Girl Scouts are trying to wean themselves from their dependency on cookie sales. With encouragement from national headquarters, councils around the nation are developing their own new fundraising ideas and programs.

The Northwest Georgia Council, for example, has adopted a new plan for raising revenue, one that requires the same entrepreneurial spirit that its youngsters show when selling mint cookies door to door. For years the council has owned a 213-acre tract of land some twenty minutes outside of downtown Atlanta; generations of Girl Scouts have camped there. In the late 1980s, however, the council acknowledged that the land was underused and that the taxes on it were draining their resources. At the same time, the national board was placing emphasis on the fact that any project undertaken by the Girl Scouts should expand and enhance the organization's image in the community. Council executive director Pat Tunno and her staff decided to convert the campgrounds into something that would accomplish that goal and generate important new revenue as well. Says Tunno, "We're good trainers, we train 3,000 people a year in this one council; we're good managers, and we're dedicated to giving good service. It seemed logical to us to build a conference center that we could use when needed but could also be leased out to the public as a revenue-producer." The Timber Ridge Conference Center, now in full operation, is used 30 percent of the time by the Girl Scouts and is leased to nonprofit organizations, private corporations, and state and local agencies for the remainder. The council has also established Timber Ridge Camp, which occupies ten acres of the conference center site. Says Tunno with a laugh, "We didn't know squat diddly about conference center management, but we brought in expertise via our board of directors, which includes one member who buys and manages hotels and another who is the vice president of a Ramada Inn." The center is managed and staffed by members of the local council, who are confident that it will become very successful. The group is also proud of the way the center was built. "We developed eleven acres," says Tunno, "but we cut down only four trees. We landscaped in the natural setting and planted it with wildflowers. I call it our testament. It's a memorial to the million kids who used that property. And it says that there's no better organization than the Girl Scouts to keep this land green."

Building on the success of the Timber Ridge experience, the Northwest Georgia Council, in 1996, developed some of the 980 acres of its Misty Mountain Program Center located several hours outside of Atlanta. Here it operates an eight-week resident camp for girls, complete with twenty-four riding horses. Like Timber

Ridge, the facility brings the Northwest Georgia Council additional revenues from other organizations who rent the property when it is not in use by the Girl Scouts.

The Nature Conservancy (TNC) boasts enormous financial resources—a land acquisition fund of over $100 million and total assets in excess of $700 million—that give it significant clout, but in the highly competitive business of land acquisition, money is not the only ingredient necessary for success. One has to be creative, and nobody beats the Conservancy for coming up with innovative strategies in pursuit of land. Some examples:

- On Shelter Island, at the eastern tip of Long Island, the Conservancy identified a large number of endangered ospreys nesting on more than 2,000 acres belonging to a hunting club. The real estate company that owned the club would not sell it separately from all the rest of the corporation's real estate. So, at a cost of almost $11 million, the Conservancy bought all of the company's holdings, including a warehouse in Florida, oil and gas leases in three separate states, and nine buildings in New York City. After converting the club into a preserve, TNC resold the rest of the purchase at a profit.
- To avoid setting off an acrimonious debate about development versus environment, associates of the Conservancy formed a dummy corporation in order to bid directly as a developer against developers for Metomkin Island, a barrier island off the coast of Virginia. The Conservancy won the bidding, bought other islands in the chain, and converted its acquisitions into what is now the spectacular natural sanctuary known as the Virginia Coast Reserve.
- In the 1980s, International Paper Company put 12,000 acres of land adjacent to Vermont's Stratton Mountain ski area up for sale. The asking price was $3.1 million, with the proviso that the purchase be made within three weeks. The U.S. Forest Service wanted to add the land to the Green Mountain National Forest but needed at least six months to raise the money. The Vermont chapter of TNC borrowed the $3.1 million from the Conservancy's revolving fund and purchased the land. When the government funds came through, the land was resold to the Forest Service for the original $3.1 million asking price plus interest, which went back into the revolving fund.

Take Risks; Tolerate Mistakes

Risk taking is not a phrase we associate with public-sector organizations. Says Ellen Schall, former director of New York's Department of Juvenile Justice (DJJ), "I think that the public imagines that the private sector is all about risks and research and development and going out on a long limb. Somehow they want the same behavior to take place in the public sector, but they're not as happy with failures. And inherent in taking risks is accepting failure. So public-sector managers need to find some way to create some protective space for their staff so they can take risks and survive." Schall lists the following ingredients as essential to creating this protective space:

- Articulation of the vision and goals of a new program by those at the top of the organization.
- Clear indication of full support for the program from those at the top.
- An organizationwide effort to solicit support for the program at all levels of the organization.
- A clear indication that, within reason, the inevitable mistakes will be tolerated and the "heat" for these mistakes will be taken at the top.

Says Jesse Doyle, former executive director of DJJ's Spofford Detention Facility, "When people make mistakes, generally they don't do everything wrong. If there are ten steps in a process, most people get more than five of them right. The key is not to dwell on what people did wrong but to focus on what they did right. That way they can get the formula right and then go forward to new horizons."

Reward Your Risk Takers

The Giraffe Project is a nonprofit foundation founded by John Graham and Ann Medlock in 1982 with their combined savings of $17.00. Its purpose is to spotlight those who promote the common good by "sticking their necks out." Giraffe encourages risks of all types, whether financial, social, or emotional. The reward to the risk taker, aside from personal satisfaction, is simple—public exposure for the cause that one is sticking one's neck out for. "Giraffe's mission," says Medlock, "is to tell people that what you do matters. You don't have to wait for an institution to do something." She adds, "There is a broad range of risk. We might discover someone who is very shy who stood up and made a fuss about something, taking a great personal risk." Giraffes come in

➡

Reward Your Risk Takers (continued)

all shapes and sizes, ranging from Celeste and David McKinley, who run a market that provides free groceries to those in need, to Gary Polhemus, a part-time actor who founded We Can, a recycling business whose sole intent is to provide financial aid to the homeless. Giraffes also include children, who have been recognized for taking action in the face of peer pressure.

Medlock and Graham's endeavors have been so successful that they have expanded their activities. What started out as effort to encourage people to take risks has grown. Today the project has a Giraffe Program curriculum in schools in forty-seven states. It has formed alliances with YMCA and YWCA Boys and Girls Clubs and the U.S. Navy.

The basic tenets of Giraffe's "neckbone approach" can be applied to any organization to maximize efficiency. They are:

1. Develop a vision
2. Do your homework
3. Change your sense of direction
4. Build a group vision
5. Communicate
6. Above all, feel free to take the necessary risks to make anything better than you found it.

Consider the Turtle

When Neil Behan was chief of the Baltimore County Police Department, his office was filled with ceramic, metal, and wooden turtles. Why the turtles? "Soon after I was made captain in the New York City police department," he explains, "I was given the planning division. My boss told me to hire and fire who I wished, but my task was to bring the department into the twentieth century. I inherited a very fine group of talented people who had been knocked down, kicked around, and abused so much that they were just leveled. My challenge was to try and get them going. While I began to push against the barriers of traditional policing, I came across the old slogan 'Consider the turtle. It makes very little progress unless it sticks its neck out.' So I had signs with that slogan posted around the division. And they were torn down and I put them up again. And guys threw darts at them. But eventually they stayed up and people started to believe. When I left New York, I figured that was the end of the turtles. What I had forgotten was that cops talk to each other. And when I took over here, there was the turtle on my stationery along with the slogan."

Innovation Can Be Fun

In their ceaseless efforts to raise funds, the people at Fairfax County's Medical Care for Children Project (MCCP) consider every idea that is brought to them, no matter how "far out" it may seem. During one of the project's board meetings, someone suggested staging a golf tournament as a means of adding to their coffers. As soon as the suggestion was made, another board member responded, "Oh, no, not another golf tournament. I would pay good money not to get involved in another golf tournament." Someone else said, "Hey, that's a great idea. Why don't we have a golf tournament that nobody goes to. People can pay for the privilege of not having to attend. If nobody shows up, it'll be a tremendous success." Thus was born the MCCP Annual Phantom Golf Tournament, an event that raises thousands of dollars for this important project. Inspired by their success, the folks at MCCP then established an Annual Phantom Costume Ball.

In turning around Webster Elementary School, Principal Cindy Cannell's first goal was to raise attendance. Taking an innovative approach, she started by making Webster a fun place to be. Said Cannell, "Kids should think, 'I don't want to miss school today because you can never tell what will happen.'" Once Cannell became "gorilla for a day," donning a gorilla suit to repay a promise made to students that she would do so if they read a certain number of books. On another occasion, in return for a student body pledge to keep themselves drug free, she agreed to let the local sheriff "arrest" her and put her in a "jail" at school.

Cannell continually implemented special programs, both planned and impromptu, designed to keep school a lively and exciting place. She used the Halloween and Christmas seasons as occasions both for fun and for food drives to benefit needy families. Students and staff came to school in outlandish costumes, and extra costumes were made available so that no one would be left out. Most popular of all the programs was Friday Theme Day. One Friday was Nerd Day, another was Crazy Hair Day, and still another Shades Day or Pajama Day. It was all designed to get a student body with a prior record of high absenteeism into the building so that education could take place. As Cannell summed it up, "I'd rather play with the kids on the playground, read stories to them in the library, or plant flowers with them in the garden," she says, "than stay in my office handling discipline cases."

Surmounting the Obstacles to Public-Sector Innovation

Alan Altshuler, director of the Kennedy School Innovations in American Government Program, and Marc Zegans, former executive director of the program, list the following characteristics that distinguish innovative public-sector organizations:

- They proceed incrementally.
- They act to alleviate problems wide recognized as urgent and are adept at explaining the connection between problem and solution.
- They are close to their clients, who send positive messages to political authorities.
- They cast their nets widely in search of support.
- They are skilled at building and sustaining networks.
- They are open to feedback.
- They are tenacious, passionately committed, and optimistic.

We've seen how the flow of new ideas both changes and revitalizes an organization. But initiating these ideas is not enough. They must also be executed, and the best way to execute them is to put power in the hands of those who can make innovation happen—those on the front line, closest to the action. It's not easy for any manager to relinquish power, and it can be a risky business, but, as we'll see in the next chapter on sharing the power, once it's done, it can bring surprising and often remarkable results.

8

SHARING THE POWER

Empowerment" is a word we hear a great deal these days. Organizations talk about the concept, but few actually put it into general practice. The organizations in this book, however, refuse to hoard power at the top or at the center but share power *down* to the front line and *out* from headquarters. What we've learned from these organizations is that where power sharing is most complete, overall performance is most astounding.

Power sharing is a tough nut to crack. "Sharing" sounds like a euphemism for "relinquishing," and in most cases it is. Relinquishing earned power is foreign to the way most of us learned to manage. It certainly is not the way most of our bosses behaved toward us. Most of us believe that power sharing is a great idea, but only insofar as *we* are the beneficiaries of that power. When suddenly we are expected to share power we have worked hard for, we tend to come up with all sorts of reasons why that is not really a very good idea at all.

The best managers have learned that hoarding power makes no sense and that so doing they cheat themselves as well as their employees. They have learned that giving the people in their organization the power to manage themselves, to manage the organization's resources, and even to manage their customers, increases the power of the organization as a whole.

Most important, the organizations we studied understand that real power, which marries responsibility with autonomy and authority, makes it possible for people at every level to respond intelligently, effectively, and quickly to the changing moment. They know that the possession of intelligence without power, which is the state of most front-line people in most organizations, is a recipe for cynicism, the fuel for all those water-cooler conversations about what the organization *should* have done.

In the following pages you will encounter a variety of cases in which top public-service managers bit the bullet, shared the power, and transformed their organizations. You will also read about one organization that was built from the start on power sharing and about the kinds of miracles it performs every day.

Get the Power Out of the Executive Suite and Away from Headquarters

In the early 1980s, the Forest Service faced two major problems. First, like most other organizations, private and public, it needed to improve productivity, quality, and service. Second, an internal survey revealed that employees felt stifled by bureaucratic controls and rules. Forest Service chief Max Peterson and associate chief Dale Robertson dealt with these problems head-on by instituting a program called the Pilot Test Study. Unlike most government programs, this pilot didn't try to solve a problem by issuing a report or by adding new policies and procedures. Instead, it eliminated organizational barriers and gave those closest to the action the power to redesign the system in order to improve performance. And, unlike most federal programs, the pilot wasn't housed in Washington.

During the first stage of the pilot, four Forest Service units were designated as participants: the Gallatin National Forest in Montana, the Mark Twain National Forest in Missouri, the Pacific Southwest Forest and Range Experiment Station in California, and the Ochoco National Forest in Oregon. In each of these places, staff and employees were given the following incentives:

- Maximum flexibility to change operating procedures within the law.
- The ability to operate with lump-sum budgets (controlled by appropriation, not by line items) to allow operational flexibility.
- Control over staffing and organizational structure.
- The power to keep whatever savings accrued from increases in productivity within the forest itself.
- Acknowledgment from top staff in Washington that risk taking would be encouraged and that failures, within reason, would be tolerated.

Having announced its commitment to decentralization and to a process in which change would be implemented from the bottom up, top management honored its word and left the pilots alone to sink, swim, or even fly. And they flew. Over the next two years, morale, spirit, commitment, and ingenuity shot skyward, with some astounding results. In the first year, there was a 10 to 15 percent increase in productivity in the pilot forests, compared with a .7 percent productivity increase in the federal government and a .6 percent increase in the private sector. Several other forests and one whole region were added to the program. Other forests not specifically designated as pilots began bootlegging innovations from the pilot units to begin making their own changes and improvements. But it was in the Ochoco National Forest that the pilot initially took the greatest leaps forward. In the first year after the program was inaugurated, Ochoco's productivity soared 25 percent, and in the second year it climbed an additional 35 percent.

The Ochoco National Forest is a big and complex business. Every year it oversees the harvest of about forty million board feet of lumber. In addition to managing timber, it manages mineral resources, watersheds, and big game, as well as fish and wildlife. The Ochoco also maintains recreational facilities and hiking, camping, and hunting programs. Employees build roads and fight fires. The Forest Service also manages several parcels inside the Ochoco, that belong to Native Americans, and that encompass tribal sites and traditional native plants. Those who run the forest must not only manage diversity, but they must manage to maintain diversity.

Share Power Face to Face

When the pilot program was launched in the Ochoco Forest, Dale Robertson, who succeeded Max Peterson as chief, flew out from Washington to kick it off, to answer questions, and to put his name, position, and enthusiasm behind the effort. Most important, Robertson was there to pass along his power symbolically to the men and women of the Ochoco. "That was the dramatic event for this forest," says Dave Rittersbacher, who was forest supervisor at the Ochoco when the pilot was launched, "having the chief come to Prineville, Oregon, and personally spell out the specific ways in which the system would be loosened up and the ways in which we would be given freedom to do our work as we saw fit. Most important, he let us know that he understood that with any innovative program comes the risk of failure and that as long as we kept learning from our experiences, failures along the way would be tolerated. He told us, in fact, that when failures did occur, he would 'take the heat.'"

True Power Sharing Involves Everyone

Within days of its selection as a pilot forest, the Ochoco's staff and employees put forth more than 700 suggestions for improvement. In the first year, the forest logged productivity savings of $177,000, money that could now be spent on forest projects. Savings came from every nook and cranny. For instance, Ochoco's administration officer, Rod Collins, targeted a $10,000 reduction on the phone bill, and workers responded by saving over $48,000 in this one area alone. Some savings came in response to clearly set targets; others resulted from the way that the pilot empowered people to think and act on their own. The cost reductions came in small bits as well as big lots. For example, a mailroom employee, on her own initiative, achieved a $100 savings by eliminating an outdated service. An assistant district ranger reduced the cost of adding a new deck onto his station by scavenging wood from an old tower that was being pulled down.

Aside from the commitment to savings, the participative approach to running the forest had other positive effects. Operating under the pilot, even Ochoco's budget and finance staff began to feel that they were part of the forest and not simply Washington's watchdogs. They adopted a campground. One day a week, using time previously devoted to dealing with red tape, they began to care for a campground whose maintenance funding had been canceled. Leaving their computers and purchase orders, they cleaned it up, and they did such a good job that the campground received the highest rating possible from the American Automobile Association.

There is no better example of the pilot at work than the Ochoco's efforts in coping with a 58,000-acre forest fire in the summer of 1990. The massive firefighting effort required four thousand people. But the really hard work began after the fire was extinguished, when the forest had to assess the damage done both by the fire itself and by the firefighters. Next, it had to plan how to harvest the remaining timber and reseed, replant, and restore the burned areas. Three environmental assessment reports on planned restoration efforts had to be researched, written, and filed. Finally, there were the public comment and appeal stages. All of this was done concurrently with the selling of the remaining usable timber before it lost additional value. The fire was extinguished in August and, thanks to the pilot spirit, the majority of the timber was sold by December. "This, for those who don't understand how long this process normally takes," says Rod Collins, "is the equivalent of setting the world land speed record. The fact that each person involved in the process had decision-making authority was what made this minor miracle possible."

By any measure, the pilot has been judged an outstanding success, one that brought home an important lesson: All too often management not only cannot solve the problem; it *is* the problem. When we asked former chief Dale Robertson to evaluate what he had learned from the pilot, he responded by stating, "Our biggest surprise came at the beginning when we asked our employees,

'What is it that's getting in your way of getting the job done? What's stifling creativity and innovation out here?' You know who they assessed as being responsible for 70 percent of it? The Forest Service. It was the managers in the Forest Service. Only 30 percent, they claimed, was due to the executive branch and Congress. And so, I think, before federal managers start griping and complaining about Congress, they better worry about the 70 percent that's on their backs that they can do something about."

Like the Forest Service, the U.S. Geological Survey (USGS) also learned that true employee involvement is a key to management success. "We are all aware that we operate within a federal bureaucracy," says the survey's public affairs officer, Don Kelly, "but here at the survey we refuse to regard the system as a barrier to achievement. The most important way we overcome this barrier is by hiring the best people possible, pointing them in the right direction, and then stepping back and giving them the freedom to do their jobs." Some specific examples:

- The survey recently produced a book that documents the goals of each of the various divisions within the agency. When it was still in draft form, the book was sent to every one of the survey's more than 10,000 employees for suggestions and comments. When all the comments were in and extensive revisions had been made based on employee input, only then was the book published.
- All of the survey's divisions hold regularly scheduled meetings with their secretarial staffs to brief them on the purpose and progress of every project within the division. Suggestions are solicited. "We want our secretaries to know," says geologist Ben Morgan, "that they are an important part of each of our programs and that their perspective and advice is important to us. Most important, we want to make it very clear that everyone in this organization regards them as professional staff."
- The greatest task facing the national mapping division involves the transfer from graphic to digital maps. The entire process is being carried out by sending teams of employees from every section of the division out into the field and giving them the decision-making power to bring this transfer about. "All of these employees," says Don Kelly, "are vital parts of what we call our idea team. When you get the people below you committed to the goals of the organization and empowered to act on these goals, you have a happy, productive work force and, not so incidentally, you have an organization that's much easier to manage."

- The geologic division has a policy of regularly bringing staff in from the field and having them swap places with management at national headquarters to give both groups and their managers a real sense of the issues from all perspectives and to allow them to make better-informed, competent decisions.

Delegate Authority to Make Change Possible

Unlike most federal agencies, in which the leadership turns over on the average of every eighteen months, the General Accounting Office (GAO) is marked by stable, long-term leadership. The agency is headed by the comptroller general of the United States, who is appointed by the president for a fifteen-year term of office. That stability is particularly critical to an agency like the GAO, where the dismissal of its head for political reasons would have a disastrous effect on the agency's critical need to change with the times.

Former comptroller general Charles A. Bowsher, who served from 1981 to 1996, has enhanced the agency's reputation for continual improvement. Perhaps Bowsher's greatest contribution was the way he made change possible by moving decision-making authority down the line and fostering a climate of full participation. Before Bowsher's tenure, GAO reports were signed only by a handful of key agency executives, and less than a dozen key executives were allowed to testify before Congress. At Bowsher's instigation, "third-echelon" managers were given broad authority to serve as the agency's focal point in dealings with Congress, from consulting with members and key Congressional staff to signing individual reports to testifying before committees. In 1994, for example, more than eighty GAO staffers represented the agency in presenting testimony. Says former assistant comptroller general Larry Thompson, "Chuck Bowsher offers a prime example of how the person at the top can affect an organization positively. This comptroller general did this by establishing and sharing his long-term view, by his commitment to a growing and changing organization, and through the way he delegated authority to everyone and then backed them up."

Bob Stone's List of Seven Foundations of Leadership

After a distinguished career at the Department of Defense, Bob Stone is now project director of the Clinton administration's National Performance Review. Following is Bob Stone's list of what a leader must be prepared to do in order to make power sharing an integral characteristic of any organization. As a leader, asserts Stone, you must be willing to:

◆▶

Bob Stone's List of Seven Foundations of Leadership (continued)

- Change your basic paradigm, how you view your part of the world. You must open yourself up to criticism and learn from it.
- Clarify your values and underlying premises.
- Take risks and make innovations that challenge tradition and current values and culture.
- Stick with change over the years to ensure it can continue without you.
- View your organization as part of a system with various stakeholders and constituents with conflicting needs, values, and power bases.
- Work across organizational lines to build support and sell ideas.
- See real power accrue to those whose job it is to help others achieve the organizational mission and goals.

Don't Chicken Out! Power Sharing Pays Off Even in High-Risk Situations

"Policing," says Neil Behan, former chief of the Baltimore County Police Department, "is a complex profession because we carry guns and have the power of arrest. We can take liberty away from people, which is their most sacred possession. And because of these factors, we've kept our police under a very rigid set of rules. What must be done is to keep the essential rules in place but free our police up sufficiently enough so they can express themselves beyond these rigid rules. With our COPE (Citizen-Oriented Police Enforcement) units, once a problem was determined, each COPE officer had the authority to act independently to address the problem in the way he best saw fit."

This was a responsibility not lightly given. Says Colonel Don Shinnamon, who headed up the COPE units, "When you empower the officer out there on the front line, it's kind of scary for you as a manager. And, believe me, mistakes are made. Don't forget, we're police. We're brought up on control. We want to know where our officers are all the time because the potential for danger in this business is so great. And there's also the fact that police work is so confrontational. We're involved in so many things that can cause complaints. So that when you put cops out there and give them free rein to solve problems, it can sure leave you uneasy. But what we understood from the beginning is that if our community policing efforts were to be based on making each COPE officer a problem solver, then we had to give them total freedom and authority to do their job."

Paul Wieber was a COPE patrol officer. Like his counterparts, he scheduled his own time and focused his activities on projects he felt were essential to fighting fear and to solving community problems. Wieber's particular interest was in establishing positive relationships with the young people in his area. He learned early on that much of the fear felt by older citizens was engendered by the presence of idle youngsters congregating on street corners, particularly in the summer months. Wieber, along with fellow COPE officers, organized a basketball league, obtained the necessary equipment, and joined the youngsters in their games. As participation in the games increased, Wieber, on his own initiative, went to the Frito-Lay Company and obtained $3,000 for t-shirts, which he presented to the youngsters. The t-shirts became cherished items. Says Wieber, "The kids wore them proudly to school and passed the word that it was the police who provided them. It's just another example of how we can get close to the kids, how we can get them to stop seeing us as a threat and have them come to trust us."

According to Behan, putting police officers like Paul Wieber out on their own requires a special kind of executive mindset. "You've got to drain the executive of his own arrogance," says the chief. "The idea that you have to be right and that you have to prove it is simply self-defeating. That doesn't mean that you don't feel strongly about your own abilities, but it means that this feeling has to be sublimated to the mission at hand." Says Don Shinnamon, "Nobody here is afraid to experiment because we know that as long as we learn from our mistakes we have the right to fail."

Placing Power at the Seat of Action Can Bring Amazing Results

The Nature Conservancy's former chief operating officer Bill Weeks recalls that when he joined the organization as director of the Indiana state chapter, he inherited a staff of five people. Weeks and his small staff realized that if they were to purchase the land that they felt needed saving within their jurisdiction, they would have to raise $10,000,000. "Up to this point," says Weeks, "Indiana had, in its entire history, only appropriated a total of $35,000 for purchasing land for preservation. We went to the Indiana legislature and asked for $5,000,000, with the proviso that we would match that sum if they committed it to us. They said yes to us because I'm sure that no one in that body had any idea that we would possibly raise that amount of money. Everyone we talked to said, 'There's no way; you don't have the experience; you've only raised $75,000 in your history in this state and this is not a good time.' But," says Weeks, "we just told ourselves we had to do it.

"We contacted every corporation in the state, set up appointments, and made our pitch, focusing on how the corporation would benefit through tax deductions and positive press. We linked up with local environmental groups and utilized many of their contacts. We made a point of visiting with every large private donor in the state and pled our case. And we worked hard to get the story of what we were attempting in every print and media outlet possible.

"In four years, " says Weeks, "we raised five million dollars and the Indiana legislature, true to their word, matched that amount. If you were to ask me to state the main reason for our success, I'd have to say it was because we were given full responsibility and authority to do whatever it took and that all of us knew we'd be given full credit once the task was done."

Power Sharing Means Placing Employee Responsibility as Close to the Customer as Possible

Power sharing entails letting front-line people manage themselves, the organization's resources, and even the customer. All too often, the men and women who meet customers face to face are in low-paying, low-status positions. In health care, for instance, the nurses responsible for the majority of patient care are rarely given management or decision-making power. Instead, they serve as hand-maidens to the physicians.

Well before its merger with the Deaconess Hospital, Boston's Beth Israel Hospital (BI) moved boldly to institute a system of primary-care nursing in which the nurse acts as the primary-care manager (as well as service provider) for a patient's entire hospital experience. At Beth Israel, each patient admitted is assigned to a registered nurse. This primary-care nurse develops a twenty-four-hour-a-day care plan for the patient and has the main responsibility for this daily care. The primary-care nurse works closely with the patient's doctor, but it is her or his responsibility to *manage* all the care that patient receives. When the nurse goes off duty he or she leaves detailed instructions for the next shift and, while off duty, is available for instant consultation through a beeper. On the next shift, the primary-care nurse checks on the patient's progress and, in consultation with the doctor, makes any necessary adjustments to the care plan.

This is a revolutionary approach, but it's logical. "Nurses," says Joyce Clifford, BI Deaconess's senior vice president for nursing and nurse-in-chief, "are the anchor that ensures that patient care remains central. They bring a continuity to caring because of their clinical knowledge combined with their relationship with the patient, family, and with other health professionals. By giving our nurses real decision-making authority, we've given them the incentive to perform at the highest level possible, have upgraded an already excellent record of patient care, and not so incidentally have, in a highly competitive market, been able to attract the best candidates in the nursing profession."

Clifford, who was responsible for the concept of primary-care nursing, also changed the role of the head nurse at the hospital. Head nurses now have full authority to make procedural changes in their units. They also interview all prospective nurses and are fully involved in the hiring process. They have been given the chief responsibility of serving as mentors to new nurses, helping them develop professionally and seeing to it that they have the resources to deliver the best patient care possible.

What has been particularly gratifying to Clifford and her nursing staff is the way that the medical center's doctors have come to value the changes in the nursing approach. It is not surprising that initially many of the doctors were opposed to the idea of giving up some of their control. They have learned, however, that their roles as doctors have been enhanced by the reliable information they receive about their patients from the primary-care nurse and the ways in which accountability for the patients well-being is now shared in a responsible and meaningful way.

Listening to Employees Leads to Productivity and Quality Improvement

The city of Phoenix has learned that empowered employees are an organization's best resource for improving productivity and quality. Phoenix aggressively seeks employee suggestions and acts on them. The city's formal suggestion program, overseen by the personnel department, elicits more than 800 suggestions annually from every level of city government. In 1995–96, 372 suggestions were submitted and 66 were implemented, at a taxpayer savings of $2 million in the first year. Some examples of suggestions over the years:

- Steve Kolicko, facilities supervisor at Sky Harbor International Airport, modified a used soft-drink machine to replace a refrigerated enclosure for a microcomputer access control panel. Savings: $7,239.
- Detective Joe Wolfer saved the city $13,724 by suggesting that applicants for the police department be required to take oral board exams before being given the psychological exams, saving the cost of examining those who fail their oral boards.
- Equbalali Charania and Dong Che Wong of the Street transportation department became the city's champion suggesters. "These two employees," says the city's former productivity and recognition administrator, Ed Schlar, "recognized the city was using national standards as far as street paving thickness was concerned. They felt that the

climate and the nature of the soils here might require us to take a real in-depth look at our paving standards. They performed some calculations that allowed us to lay pavement one inch less thick. One inch translates to over $50,000 a mile. So we're talking about $1.2 million in savings just through that one employee suggestion alone."

In 1991, as the nation entered a deep recession, Phoenix met the challenge by turning to its workers for suggestions on how to meet the budget shortfall. Within days, 900 suggestions poured in. Even before they were all reviewed, administrators discovered that the suggestions contained enough practical strategies to generate savings that would preserve at least 250 jobs.

"We had at least a couple of suggestions," says Ed Schlar, "where people actually recommended the elimination of their jobs as a viable cost-saving measure. In both cases, in fact, we eliminated those positions at the end of the year. But we made a commitment that these people weren't going to lose out and we found comparable positions for them."

Phoenix's Guide for Employee Suggestions

The employee suggestion has been the butt of jokes for sixty years or more. But not in Phoenix, where suggestions from the basis for constant improvement. Here are excerpts from the guidelines for suggestions published by the city of Phoenix:

The City of Phoenix is a recognized leader in productivity and generating cost savings as a result of employee participation. To maintain that leadership role, we need a continuing flow of fresh ideas to increase efficiency and reduce costs. It is our goal to continually improve our operations and the services we provide to the people of our City. Your suggestions will help us to do this.

We invite you to join your fellow employees in contributing to the Employee Suggestion Program. Each accepted suggestion may be eligible for a cash award. Top award suggestions receive the "Gold Coin" award plus cash. You might find that there is "Gold" in your ideas.

What is a "suggestion"? A "Suggestion" is a written original idea proposed by an employee of the City of Phoenix to the Employee Suggestion Committee that clearly suggests a specific method to do any job or procedure better, quicker, easier, safer, or at less cost.

How do I get started? The best place to look for suggestions is right in your own department. There are always better ways of doing things. If you analyze each step you will find a better way.

●➔

Phoenix's Guide for Employee Suggestions

How do I submit a suggestion?   Suggestion forms are available at conveniently located ESP display boxes. Print or type the required information, being careful to clearly state both the current situation and your solution. Include additional suggestion details, pictures, sketches or other back-up data whenever possible.

What happens to my suggestion after it has been submitted?   As soon as your suggestion is received by the Employee Suggestion Committee it is date stamped and given a number. This number is for use in locating your suggestion when an inquiry is made. Upon receipt of your suggestion you will be sent a letter of acknowledgment. Also, your suggestion will be reviewed by the Employee Suggestion Committee Coordinator and then forwarded to the proper evaluating department(s).

What comes next?   Each suggestion submitted is assigned by the evaluating department(s) to a technically qualified employee for evaluation. The department(s) have twenty-one (21) days to assess the suggestion and respond to the Employee Suggestion Committee. If additional review time is needed, the department(s) notify the ESP Office and the suggester is informed of the suggestion's status.

When will I hear whether my suggestion has been adopted?   You will hear in writing within 60 days of the date your suggestion is received by the Employee Suggestion Committee. If evaluation or implementation of your suggestion is a complex process, it may take longer than 60 days to receive your answer. When this is the case you will be kept advised of the status of your suggestion.

What happens if I submit a suggestion which is not adopted?   After final determination by the Employee Suggestion Committee that a suggestion is ineligible for an award, a letter is sent to the suggester giving a full explanation as to why the idea was not adopted.

What kind of awards can I win?   There are four types of awards:

- Cash Awards—up to $2,500
- Certificates of Award (Signed by Mayor and City Manager)
- Certificate of Commendation (Signed by Mayor and City Manager)
- Plaques

How are cash awards determined?   Awards for suggestions with verifiable monetary value will be 10 percent of the estimated first year's net savings or net increase in revenues. Awards will range from a minimum of $25 to a maximum net award of $2,500.

Awards for suggestions which are of intangible value are determined according to their impact on City operations and range from $25 to $300.

Empower People to Work Together

In 1990, rising costs within Phoenix's public works department drove its expenses beyond bid projections. There was a real possibility that the department would lose the contract it had won in competitive bidding. Analysis revealed that equipment maintenance costs were the primary culprit. The real problem was that, historically, the equipment management division and the solid waste division, which was responsible for refuse collection, did not work together. The refuse collection drivers complained that their trucks weren't fixed correctly, while the mechanics complained that the drivers didn't take proper care of the trucks on the road. In order to bring down maintenance costs, drivers and mechanics would have to start working together. Otherwise refuse collection would have to go out for bid again, and equipment maintenance might, for the first time, have to go out for bid as well.

Once the two departments realized their joint dilemma, mechanics and drivers began working to solve the problems. A twelve-person team of mechanics launched a pilot program called ROAM (Reduce Operations and Maintenance Costs). They began by identifying and recording their trucks' repair needs and by developing new ideas for efficiency and putting them in writing for all to see. They met regularly with drivers to compare their findings and discuss ways to work together to solve recurring problems. For instance, drivers convinced mechanics that they, the drivers, could handle the daily walk-around inspections before taking the trucks out. This eliminated duplication of effort. Drivers, in turn, looked at ways they could reduce maintenance. They started to take better care of the trucks in their possession. Some drivers even developed more efficient routes in order to reduce fuel and maintenance costs. The drivers have now standardized their best practices, and the mechanics now use rebuilt parts rather than costly new parts whenever possible.

Give Power to the Team!

The San Diego Zoological Society discovered that it can multiply the benefits of power sharing by giving authority not only to individuals but to front-line teams. Instead of organizing itself into conventional bird, mammal, and reptile departments, the zoo created bioclimatic zones such as savannas and rain forests. Teams made up of individuals from various disciplines—animal keepers, horticulturists, curators, maintenance and construction workers—were put together to manage the animal and plant resources of these zones and to keep them operating efficiently.

The teamwork concept enables employees to test new ideas and approaches. A seven-member team, for example, was put in charge of the zoo's $7 million, three-acre African jungle exhibit called Tiger Run. The project became an enormous success with visitors and employees. Absenteeism and complaints among employees connected with the project were almost nonexistent.

Giving teams managerial power has proven so successful that director Douglas Myers and general manager Art Risser have formed crossfunctional teams to solve specific problems relating to the zoo's activities. One team was given the task and the authority of reducing the zoo's water consumption by 10 percent. Water use is a major issue in an arid area of a state plagued by several years of drought. By working together and sharing ideas, the conservation team reduced water consumption by 40 percent.

"Giving authority to teams," says Art Risser, "has become the secret of our management style. We just set some modest goals and go away and let people shock and surprise us."

Sharing the Power Leads to Better Customer Service

The school-based management program in Rochester, New York, has been a genuine success. This program is designed to move power away from traditional centralized authority and place it in the hands of those most closely involved in a student's educational experience. Every elementary, middle, and high school in Rochester has a management team of teachers, parents, administrators, students, and community members who decide on issues that relate to instruction, student performance, school environment, and improvement. All of the management team's decisions are made by consensus and are binding on school staff provided that the decision is within the authority of the school.

Each school's management team is required to prepare an annual school improvement plan for student performance. The teams are also required to hold a town meeting to present their plan for the current year and an evaluation report on their success in meeting the goals of the previous year's plan.

"Being a part of a school-based management team is a wonderful experience," says Barbara Hasler, a veteran teacher at Rochester's Monroe Middle School. "I feel truly empowered. In the past we've all felt that all the decisions were coming from the central office. Now we have a lot to say about what happens. That's terribly important because it's the parents, the staff, and the teachers who know more about the students and everything that goes on in their building than anyone else. We now have a really effective method for making change. We've encouraged people who have been previously unrepresented in school decisions—members of the black and

Hispanic communities—to join our teams. And that, along with being able, for the first time, to work closely with administration allows all of us to understand everyone's concerns and to address them."

Thanks to the school-based management approach, block scheduling has been instituted at the Monroe School. Under this system, all classes are scheduled for one-and-a-half hours duration instead of the traditional forty-five minutes, a change that allows teachers to cover subjects in much greater depth and eliminates much of the time that was wasted by students continually passing from one classroom to another.

Due to another innovation worked out through school-based management, Monroe students now take two core subjects (chosen from English, math, social studies, and science) a semester. This has been a salvation for many students, for if they fail one of these subjects in the first semester, there is room in their second semester schedule to get significant remedial help in that subject. The school-based management team at the Monroe School oversees staff development. The entire team surveys the school's faculty to determine their needs and then considers how best to see that these needs are met.

Says the Monroe Middle School's principal, Robert Pedzich, "Teachers here have come to believe that they can really make a difference. They can control what takes place in this building. I can't do it alone and I have no interest in doing it alone. The students are the customers in this building and through school-based management the teachers and I have the power to deliver the best programs we can to our youngsters."

Absolute Power Sharing Plus Strict Accountability Equals Limitless Results

Empowerment comes in many forms, and sometimes it comes in a form that no management expert would recognize. The Delancey Street Foundation of San Francisco, California, does not look or operate like any other nonprofit, nor does it resemble any business or government agency. Started in 1971 by four former alcohol and drug addicts with $1,000 borrowed from a loan shark, Delancey Street operates a residential treatment program for criminals, alcoholics, and drug addicts. Today there are more than one thousand residents in five campuses nationwide, and the program, in the opinion of Karl Menninger, founder and chairman of the Menninger Clinic, "is the best and most successful rehabilitation program I have studied in the world."

Delancey Street has a professional staff of one, president Mimi Silbert. It asks for and receives no government or foundation grants.

Residents earn their way to rehabilitation primarily by running ten different businesses, including a restaurant, a catering business, a moving company, a construction firm, an auto repair shop, an antique restoration firm, a printing plant, and Christmas tree lots. In addition, the foundation is one of the nation's largest distributors of imprinted hats and shirts to college bookstores. Together, these businesses generated $6 million in sales in 1990.

The businesses are run by residents, managed by residents, and controlled by residents. Residents sell, produce, keep the books, prepare the bids, and serve the customers. Occasionally, problems crop up that require additional experience and expertise. Then the residents call on board members or graduates to advise them.

Total empowerment of all residents is the secret of Delancey Street's success. But that empowerment is built on a strict set of standards. Applicants to the program are accepted or rejected by a team of veteran residents, based on a set of clear rules. Each resident, for example, must agree to stay in the program for two years, to give up drugs and alcohol, to give up the clothes and style of street and prison life, even to cut ties with friends and family for an initial period. Those who violate any of the rules are immediately dropped from the program. There are no exceptions; even one of Delancey Street's founders was expelled.

The program's boot-camp discipline from 7:00 A.M. to 11:00 P.M. is maintained with relentless peer pressure. As the residents succeed at work and as they build honest relationships with others, they earn small rewards, such as moving up a notch in their jobs or moving from a dorm to a semiprivate room. Then they take on the responsibility (and achievement) of helping newer residents. Or, as Delancey Street Foundation's president Mimi Silbert summarizes the process, "First you succeed, then you can hope to succeed."

There is no question that the key to Delancey Street's remarkable accomplishment, aside from the guiding hand of Mimi Silbert, is its total focus on empowerment and self-reliance. For instance, when the foundation started up its campus in New Mexico, the new site was staffed with ten residents from the San Francisco campus. Silbert selected them for this task from among that group she calls "tweeners," residents who had served a year or more in the program and who were neither star performers nor in trouble. She gathered the group together and gave them a pep talk about how important this program was to everyone at the foundation. Then she delegated the jobs. "Who here has ever cooked?" she asked. When someone responded affirmatively, she said, "Okay, you're in charge of the kitchen." The rest of the work was parceled out just that way. And it worked. These ten people got the project up and running and have since built up to 150 residents. In the process, they have completed the construction of a sewer system and water treatment plant and have built dormitories and a 40,000-square-foot business complex. All this, and not an MBA or even a high-school diploma among them.

Making Power Sharing a Reality

Rod Collins, administrative officer of the U.S. Forest Service's Ochoco National Forest, lists the following prerequisites for making power sharing an integral part of an organization's culture:

- Understand that true power sharing will not be achieved unless it is visibly supported from the top levels of the organization.
- Move decision-making authority as far down the line of the organization as possible.
- Give those closest to the action the power to make day-by-day decisions.
- Tolerate mistakes. Let those within your charge know that you will share in the consequences when mistakes are made.
- Operate with the understanding that true power sharing means sharing real power. Don't hold back. Give people the genuine authority to be in charge of their world.
- Establish a system for soliciting suggestions from employees. Treat each suggestion seriously. Respond to every suggestion as quickly as possible. Act upon those that you feel have merit.
- Recognize and reward all employees whose suggestions add to the effectiveness of your organization.
- Wherever possible, spread the decision-making authority to front-line teams. Multiply the benefit of these teams by comprising them of individuals from various departments and disciplines within the organization.
- Bring your customers into the action. Solicit ideas from them and act quickly upon their suggestions.

Power Sharing Means It's Their Baby

"We believe in teamwork," says the Children's Museum of Indianapolis's executive vice president Paul Richard. "We use teams to work on issues, plans, and problems all the time. And we make sure that every level of the organization is included. We've put interns in charge of a particular project. Everyone here feels a part of what we do and what's going on." That's why when some new exhibits open, the museum staff participates in a special ceremony: Volunteers and staff all sign their names on the back of the exhibit. In fact, when the museum's new CineDome Theater opened, everyone assembled to sign a special wall on this new addition.

Says museum president Peter Sterling, "We strive to avoid being bureaucratic at all costs. I am in and out of everything. I function as a cheerleader, encouraging people to be innovative, to change, to come up with their best. I get involved to the degree that staff knows I care, but no more. I never tell them how to do their work. We establish goals as teams and work them out with managers. The way it turns out is their baby."

"A lot of the time," he continues, "management does not know the details of what is going on around here. We don't have to because people are empowered to do their jobs. I walked into a doctor's office and while in the waiting room watched a videocassette that was telling the story of some great programs at a museum. And it was ours! I went back to the office and found out that we were using a promotional piece and had distributed it to more than 2,000 dentists' and doctors' offices. It was wonderful. Once a month I am in some place like a supermarket and someone will come up and tell me how much they enjoyed such-and-such a program. I thank them, go back to the office, find out whose program it is, and write them a handwritten note congratulating them. I couldn't possibly keep track of thousands of programs per year. I don't have to— all I have to do is lead the cheers."

B y now it should be obvious that everything boils down to people. The best strategies in the world won't work unless the organization makes it clear that its people are its most important asset. This attitude begins with training people properly, giving them the tools to carry out all that you expect of them. As we'll see in the next chapter, it also depends on acknowledging their contributions, large and small, and finding every way possible to celebrate and reward their commitment and accomplishments.

9

VALUING PEOPLE

Our top-performing nonprofits and public agencies hire from the same talent pool as business organizations. They cannot afford to pay their employees as much as they would get in most corporations. They have few cash incentives to offer. Yet their people often outperform their business counterparts.

The outstanding agencies we studied fuel performance by developing, supporting, and rewarding their employees' commitment rather than by trying to control people into giving their best. All of these organizations have developed a range of attitudes, habits, programs, and strategies to get the most from their people and to enable their employees and volunteers to get the most from their work experience. These organizations display the following characteristics:

They respect people.   They listen to everyone, treat everyone's ideas seriously, and, whenever possible, eliminate the trappings of rank and station.

They encourage their people.   They constantly coach and encourage their people, thank them, praise them, and reward them for accomplishments both large and small.

They develop their people.   They create organizations that promote employees' learning growth. They match people with jobs they can grow into. They provide training programs designed not only to support productivity but to foster the professional and personal growth of everyone in the organization.

They challenge their people.   They set high standards knowing that people are capable of more when more is expected.

They don't settle for satisfactory; they demand the extraordinary. To make this happen, they give their people the power, authority, autonomy, and responsibility to do the job.

They care about people. They don't have two classes of people—managers and workers. They have one class—owners.

In the following pages, you will see how all these characteristics pay off for our vanguard organizations and will encounter the strategies they use to encourage committed people to become top performers.

Trust and Respect Are Vital

Many managers could perform very well if it weren't for people—independent, inventive, unpredictable people. Learning to value people, to create situations in which they can contribute at peak, is the most difficult job a manager has. For lessons in how to do this toughest of jobs, we went to a manager who did his job under the very toughest conditions—inside a federal prison.

The Federal Bureau of Prisons is the fastest-growing segment of the federal government. In this giant system, one prison, McKean Federal Correctional Institution, stands out. Located in the rolling hills around Bradford, Pennsylvania, the low buildings of the medium-security prison resemble a college campus, if you ignore the chain-link fence, the electronically controlled double doors, and the razor wires.

We went to McKean in response to a letter sent by an inmate to Tom Peters. The letter claimed that the prison was managed as well as any business. At McKean, we met Warden (read CEO) Dennis Luther, a mild-mannered veteran of the Bureau of Prisons. We soon discovered that whereas the stereotypical warden controls through fear, Luther led through respect and trust.

The men incarcerated at McKean are criminals. Everyone on both sides of the bars is clear about that. They get no favors, no special treatment. What Luther provided was a facility run on the basis of respect for human dignity as well as respect for law and order.

"Prisoners are sent to McKean *as* punishment," says Luther. "They are not sent here *for* punishment. The punishment is to live without family, friends, work, freedom. I expect my guards and all prison personnel to be responsive to inmate requests and concerns and, more importantly, to always make decisions that are just and fair. I expect them to be courteous and professional in all their dealings with the inmates, regardless of their behavior."

Treating inmates as customers is certainly not the way most prisons operate. But during our visits to McKean, where we met with both inmates and staff, we came to applaud the daring and effectiveness of the prison's management approach. "Our job is to manage the inmates while they're in jail," says one associate warden. "The old way of managing inmates by force and intimidation doesn't work. If you back a person into a corner and kick him and kick him and kick him, he will kick back. You've already backed a person into the corner by putting him in prison. Remember, these inmates allow us to run the prison. Anytime they want to take it over they can."

At the heart of the way Luther led McKean was his staff's commitment to listening to the inmates. The prison conducted regular "town hall" meetings at which inmates could talk directly to the warden about issues and concerns. Quarterly surveys were conducted, giving inmates additional opportunities to air their concerns and submit their suggestions. Guards, staff members, and prison executives were encouraged to "hang out" in the cafeteria during lunchtime so that they would be available to answer inmates' questions on an informal basis. One manager puts it simply. "The job," he says, "is to listen to the inmates."

Respect for inmates was evident in other ways. The warden was highly visible and accessible to both staff and inmates. Most important, he saw that deeds lived up to words. In every federal prison, for example, there are periodic shakedowns or searches of inmate cells. For security reasons, guards are required to shake down a certain number of cells every shift. In most prisons, the guards tear a cell apart, leaving the inmates to put it back together again. Luther required his guards to leave each cell exactly as they found it.

Dennis Luther was obviously a maverick, and his philosophy was not widely adopted. But by treating inmates with respect and allowing them to earn trust, he built an organization that served inmates, staff, and taxpayers as well as or better than any other correctional facility in the nation. The American Correctional Association gave the facility a 99.3 accreditation rating, one of the highest among the entire Bureau of Prisons.

Respect Passes the Toughest Test

Respect for inmates as people was fundamental to the success of McKean. In a time when politicians and voters call for a halt to the "coddling" of prisoners, McKean was hailed as the best in the system—for taxpayers as well as for inmates—in some measure *because* prisoners were treated with respect. Even though it was badly overcrowded and housed violent criminals, McKean only cost taxpayers approximately $15,370 a year per inmate, compared to a federal average of $21,350 per inmate.

Respect In Action

Following are some of Luther's twenty-eight beliefs, compiled during his years as a federal warden and posted throughout the prison:

- Inmates are sent to prison as punishment and not for punishment.
- Correctional workers have a responsibility to ensure that inmates are returned to the community no more angry or hostile than when they were committed.
- Be responsive to inmate requests for action or information. Respond in a timely manner and respond the first time an inmate makes a request.
- Be dependable when dealing with inmates. If you say you are going to do something, do it.
- Never, never lie to an inmate.
- Don't impose rules, regulations, or regimentation that cannot be reasonably tied to the need to maintain order and security.

Imagine how such a code of beliefs might work in an open work environment.

Valuing People Means Not Leaving Them in the Lurch

By 1989, after seven years at the helm of New York's Department of Juvenile Justice (DJJ), commissioner Ellen Schall felt she had achieved what she had set out to do and was ready to move on to new challenges outside the agency. Soon after she announced her decision, she organized a retreat, at which the executive staff began working together to address all the issues associated with the transfer of authority. For a public-sector organization, it was a bold and unusual step. Says Tom Gilmore, vice president of the Wharton Center for Applied Research and an authority on succession issues, "Private-sector executives have more authority and discretion to hire consultants and sign off other planning expenditures for succession planning than do public-sector leaders. In the public sector, there are issues around discretion and there are hoops to go through that make it difficult and so most public-sector organizations just don't plan for succession."

Gilmore joined Schall and her staff at the retreat, and together they began addressing all that needed to be done to make sure that the transition would be as smooth as possible. The staff knew that the transfer of authority would be a long and difficult process and that, given the political nature of the appointment process, there was no guarantee of success. But they also knew that if they failed to try, they would be abandoning the many achievements their agency had realized.

There were two obvious candidates to succeed Ellen Schall. One was Rose Washington, director of the DJJ's Spofford Detention Facility. The other was assistant director Kathy Feely. When Feely, who had just had a baby, took herself out of the running, the staff began focusing on ways they could help Washington prepare for possible new responsibilities. Says Tom Gilmore, "Traditionally, there is so much fear among public-sector executives about being a lame duck that they hide their intentions to leave. If Ellen had not shared her intentions, Rose would not have had the opportunity to imagine herself in the position and get herself psychologically ready to do the job."

The DJJ's executive staff spent almost a year in the succession planning process. Schall and her assistants spent a great deal of time preparing Rose Washington, sharing with her all of the challenges facing the agency and their experience in dealing with these challenges. They made sure that Washington was given increased exposure inside and outside the agency. Schall and other veteran personnel used the political influence they had acquired over the years to help make certain that Washington's appointment as the new director would take place.

None of this was easy for Rose Washington, who knew she was replacing a respected and well-liked leader. "I took the job," she says, "because it gave me the opportunity to build on what we'd accomplished at DJJ and because I had my own vision of new paths for the organization. The most difficult part was dealing with the way people would say, 'Ellen didn't do it that way.' I had to be strong enough to follow my own vision."

There was also the issue of finding a suitable replacement for Washington as director of Spofford. After many consultations with staff and workers, Jesse Doyle was selected. "When Jesse Doyle succeeded me," says Washington, "I told him, 'I don't want you to do just what Rose Washington did. You bring your own ideas and vision and use them to build on what you find at Spofford. If you see some system in place that doesn't work—change it.'" Says Doyle, "I still stand in the shadow of Rose because she casts a giant shadow. When people say to me, 'Rose didn't do it that way,' I suggest that we talk about the way she did it and the way I intend to do it and come up with the best of both worlds."

According to Tom Gilmore, "The succession process at DJJ was successful because of their ability to address the painful issues. Their concern for their organization led them to do the necessary planning, but they did it with a lot of understanding of how it felt to be in the other person's position and they used their skill in being able to discuss difficult issues between them." Ellen Schall puts it this way. "Too often in government," she says, "everything you worked so hard to put in place is dismantled by the next group. It's so satisfying to me to know that all we did together for seven years is in the hands of people who shared the work and helped shape the vision."

Strategies for Succession

Here, taken from a paper written by Tom Gilmore and Michael J. Austin, dean of Social Work at the University of Pennsylvania, are four key strategies for a departing leader and his or her organization.

Plan the Final Months in Office Carefully.   Meet with the staff to review their collective agenda. Make sure that each important agenda item has an advocate to carry it forward. Talk with key individuals both inside and outside the organization and strategize ways to link these individuals with the organization's incoming leader.

Promote Continuity.   The departure of a leader is commonly marked by a farewell party or some such ceremony. Use that occasion as a public opportunity for staff and others to demonstrate commitments to the mission of the organization. Use it also to review past achievements and future goals and to reinforce the notion that the importance of the organization's mission lies above the interests or presence of any one leader.

Make the "Lame Duck" Period as Brief as Possible.   Once the date for a leader's departure is set and a successor has been named, it is important that the leader departs within a relatively short period of time (a month or two). The potential for ambivalent feelings between the departing leader and the successor and confusion among staff is too great when longer transition periods take place.

Use the Succession Period as a Time to Allow All Management to Reevaluate Their Organizational and Personal Goals.   Inevitably the executive's departure stirs up the thoughts of other members of the management team about leaving. One strategy that puts a positive spin on this issue is to gather managers in a retreat during the succession period. Have each manager write a scenario of his or her life a year or so hence, on the assumption that they had accepted an excellent job offer from outside the organization. In this way, each has to imagine leaving, reflect on his or her strengths and areas for improvement, how those might be viewed in other organizational settings, and different ways of creating opportunities to market themselves. Also, by thinking about leaving, they put themselves in a better position to reflect on what they find particularly valuable in staying. "Resigning" and "re-signing up" are closely linked.

Source: "Executive Exit: Multiple Perspectives on Managing the Leadership Transition," by Michael J. Austin and Thomas N. Gilmore.

Value People by Investing In Their Education

A few years ago, Beth Israel Hospital's surgeon-in-chief, Dr. William Silen, was in China delivering a lecture to a group of Chinese physicians. "I was taking questions," says Silen, "and I responded to one query by answering, 'I don't know.' My response was followed by uproarious laughter. The reason for the laughter was that the surgeons in the audience had never heard a fellow doctor say, 'I don't know.'" Silen concludes, "There are many things that doctors do not know."

A spirit of inquiry and a passion for learning are integral parts of the Beth Israel culture, which has carried over to the recently formed Beth Israel Deaconess Medical Center. BI conducts an extraordinary number of training courses and programs. As a teaching facility, one of its primary responsibilities is to train future doctors, and more than 675 interns, residents, and postgraduate fellows receive training at the medical center each year in medicine, surgery, pathology, and other medical specialties. "In addition to educating new physicians," says president/CEO David Dolins, "nearly 1,200 students are trained in health professions ranging from nursing and social work to physical, respiratory, and occupational therapy. Dietetic interns and students in pharmacy, medical technology, and radiologic technology also receive part of their clinical education at Beth Israel Deaconess."

At the medical center, education goes far beyond the transfer of complex technical skills. Says obstetrician/gynecologist-in-chief Dr. Benjamin Sachs, "I often feel daunted by the challenge of taking on a resident who will still be in practice in the year 2020. I can educate students about the physiology of disease and the mechanisms of the disease process. I can teach the best standard of care that is known today. But, most importantly, I want to see that they assume a work habit that encourages self-education. That is really the only way to guarantee that a physician will be good now, but even better in the year 2020."

Before its merger, Beth Israel designed and instituted a special eight-week, hands-on training program for first-year medical students that focuses on caring for the whole patient. The program's designer, Liebe Kravitz, chief of gerontology and medical education, explains, "Medical students don't usually have responsibilities for patient care until their third year. This course enables them to interact with patients and their families, and along with physicians, nurses, and social workers, attend geriatric rounds. I want these future physicians to understand what it is like for these patients and families and to confront their own feelings of sadness about disability and death. How do you deal with the family around issues of grief and loss? Do the rich and poor get the same kind of medical care?" Dr. Thomas Delbanco, director of the division of general medicine and primary care, says, "For years the emphasis of training young physicians focused on specializing—looking at smaller and smaller parts of the body. We sensed a need for doctors who could take care of the whole patient again."

BI Deaconess's education program for nurses, which takes place in its Center for the Advancement of Nursing Practice, is regarded by many in the medical profession as the best in the nation. The center conducts programs in professional and leadership development, sponsors distinguished scholar lectures, and conducts an international exchange and special studies program. It provides sessions for nurses on subjects ranging from "Management Development" to "Restoring the Value of Caring" to "Creating a Climate for Nursing Excellence."

Education at the hospital isn't limited to doctors and nurses. There is also a sophisticated and comprehensive training program open to all employees, whether they work in a clerical unit, the laundry room, a research laboratory, or an administrative office. It begins with an orientation program, mandatory for all new employees. It includes management training, work-team training, stress-management training, time-management training, and training in special areas such as maternity, disability, or terminal illness. The program includes courses and seminars designed to enhance employees' personal growth as well as practical ones like "Managing Your Resources," "English as a Second Language," and "Planning and Paying for College." In addition, there is a special "Be Well" health-promotion program offering classes in such subjects as smoking cessation, nutrition, and weight control.

BI Deaconess's senior vice president of corporate communications J. Anthony Lloyd stresses the importance of wide-ranging education when he recounts a story of a member of the housekeeping staff who, while cleaning a room, was asked by a female patient who had just had a mastectomy if the cleaning woman thought the patient's husband would still want to go to bed with her. "Our employee," says Lloyd, "was trained on just how to deal with such a question and was able to give great comfort to the patient. That's what training is all about." Dr. Mitch Rabkin, CEO of Caregroup Inc., the medical center's parent organization, sums up the power of the learning organization: "Each of us is a student and remains so year after year, just as each is a teacher. Presumably we get better in each role. And that's what characterizes this medical center. Through training, we continually address such issues as: How can we all perform better? How can we better serve our customers? How can we feel better about ourselves?"

Leadership That Puts People First

While he was president/CEO of Beth Israel Hospital, Dr. Mitchell Rabkin earned a reputation for getting the most out of staff and employees in every area of his organization. We asked a number of BI physicians and employees to list the traits that they feel best characterized their leader. Here is a composite of their comments:

- He is a teacher who demands everyone put his or her best argument forward. He will take the opposite perspective to ensure that all the possibilities are explored.
- He is intolerant of sloppiness and carelessness.
- He continually demonstrates trust in people and gives them the freedom to do their jobs. He also devotes considerable effort to defining what each person's job is. The result is a loose hierarchy in which people are able to be flexible and responsive.
- He wants people who are "lucky," because they have a sense for what to do when the "breaks" appear.
- He is funny and uses humor to take the edge off a situation and loosen folks up so they can get back to work. (Rabkin once included detailed instructions in his physician newsletter on how to carve a turkey. It was a skill that physicians must, he observed, be sure to hone lest BI's reputation suffer at Thanksgiving.)
- He is egalitarian. He closed down the doctors' private lunch room and made them eat with everyone else. He also refused to add a "luxury wing" for VIPs, choosing instead to bring all the beds up to luxury grade.
- He continues to "connect" with everyone in the organization. He is as comfortable and credible with housekeepers as he is with his surgeon-in-chief.

Treat Volunteers as Staff

Many of the organizations we studied are characterized by the way they treat their volunteers. They set high performance standards for volunteers, and they value them for their dedication to the mission. At the Children's Museum of Indianapolis, kids are the customers, the museum's reason for being; and, unlike any other organization we visited or researched, kids make up the core of the volunteer staff. The museum has 650 young volunteers. Volunteers serve as guides, help plan and erect exhibits, contribute ideas for programs and activities, and serve as a sounding board for staff.

"We are the only organization I know of," says museum president Peter Sterling, "that trains many of its volunteers as well as it does its staff." All of the museum's young volunteers go through the Museum Apprentice Program, which informs them how the museum works in general. Once the apprenticeship training is completed, each youngster receives detailed training in a topic area of his or her choice, be it a specific gallery, activity, or science. Through special classes and demonstrations, each youngster also receives training designed to teach communication and interpersonal skills.

Once a youngster completes the program, he or she is required to work at the museum at least two times a month. Trainees must commit to working in one area of the museum for at least six months, after which they can transfer to another if they wish. The entire process is rigorous, and the young trainees are closely supervised and evaluated. "Teaching volunteers to accept real responsibility may, in fact," says Sterling, "be the most important lesson we give them."

Among the tangible benefits the trainees receive are free admission to the museum, a 15 percent discount in museum stores, and invitations to museum apprentice parties and the annual volunteer recognition event. But for most trainees, the intangible benefits are more important. "The training I received," says one young graduate of the program, "taught me much more than how to guide people through the museum. It taught me how to deal with people's concerns, how to explain things clearly and, best of all, how to help make the museum a better place for kids my age."

The Girl Scouts' List of Tips for Recruiting Volunteers

Almost one million adults are responsible for keeping the Girl Scouts of the U.S.A. ticking, and only 1 percent of these adults are paid. The rest are volunteers who are attracted to the organization not only by the desire to help girls but by the way they are valued. Here are their tips for recruiting volunteers:

- Remember that the best volunteer recruiters are volunteers who are happy.
- Be aware that people are attracted by appeals that are positive, honest, and enthusiastic.
- Be interested in your volunteers and what makes them happy. Be flexible in matching volunteers to the right jobs.
- Don't overrecruit—volunteers may lose interest if they have signed up to help and there isn't a job for them to do.
- Recognize volunteers' efforts.
- Assure potential volunteers that they will be provided with adequate training and supervision.

➤➤

The Girl Scouts' List of Tips for Recruiting Volunteers (continued)

- Remember that you are trying to remove people's reasons to say no, not twist their arms into volunteering.
- Avoid "first warm body through the door" methods of recruitment. If you can't get the right person, don't take anybody.
- Always offer a job description—even if it is a simple, one-sentence sketch of the work to be performed. This way, both you and the volunteer are more likely to understand the assignment.
- Always recruit volunteers on the basis of service to girls, not the needs of the Girl Scouts. People work for people, not things.

The Girl Scouts List of Why Volunteers Remain Committed

- They feel appreciated.
- They can see that their presence makes a difference.
- There is a chance for advancement.
- There is opportunity for personal growth.
- They receive private and public recognition.
- They feel capable of handling the tasks offered.
- There is a sense of belonging and teamship among co-workers.
- They are involved in the administrative process, like problem solving, decision making, and objective setting.
- They recognize that something significant is happening because the group exists.
- Their personal needs are being met.

Let Everyone Know the Value You Place on Training

At the General Accounting Office, an agency that leaves its footprints on almost every piece of federal legislation, education is serious business, and the GAO finds a variety of ways to let its staff, employees, and outsiders know how committed it is to the training process. The GAO's Training Institute provides thousands of hours of training each year. Perhaps the best indicator of how serious the GAO is about training is the location of its Training Institute, which the agency has placed on the executive floor of its national headquarters in Washington, D.C., right down the hall from the comptroller general's office.

Hunger—Speed—Weight

Valuing people begins with hiring only the best. The management staff at New York's Department of Juvenile Justice realizes that a key to success in any organization lies in hiring the best people possible and then training them thoroughly. The department's hiring procedures are guided by principles put forth by John Isaacson, head of a Boston executive search firm. Here are the three main considerations that Isaacson identifies as essential in the hiring process:

Hunger. What drives a person? Is this person's sense of his/herself tied to the need to accomplish something at work?

Speed. Can the person learn quickly? Can she or he sort through quantities of material and frame the issues? What does he or she hesitate to tackle? Is this person intuitive about people? And one of our favorite questions—can she or he juggle a number of balls at the same time?

Weight. How does the person handle authority—above, below, and sideways? Can he or she tell the truth? And hear it?

Make Sure That Training Is a Continual Process

The best organizations not only educate every employee in every way they can, they also understand that education is a continual process. From the moment an individual is accepted into the Salvation Army as a potential career officer until that career comes to an end, education is an essential part of his or her working life. Every officer is required to attend and to graduate from one of the army's four two-year officers' training schools. Although much of the curriculum focuses on theological subjects, courses also place great emphasis on managerial training, particularly as it relates to service delivery. The school's standards are high. Those who don't measure up are dropped from the program. Those who do graduate are commissioned as lieutenants in the Salvation Army and enter a five-year period of extensive on-the-job training.

Throughout their careers, officers move every three to six years. Each time an officer assumes a new post, he or she receives training for the challenges of that post. Says Major Tom Jones, national secretary for community relations, "Each district has its own distinct problems and issues that need to be managed. What works in Iowa probably won't work in Chicago. Our territorial offices do everything they can to assign the right person to the right post. But it still requires training." Divisional commanders are responsible for seeing that all of the officers under their charge receive training directly related to the challenges of their specific jobs and the locales in which they are operating. Special institutes and seminars are held in each region for this purpose, and attendance by Army officers is compulsory. "This organization has always understood," says Major Jones, "that education is a lifelong process. Our officers' training schools do a marvelous job, but no education is complete unless it includes on-the-job training and is conducted as a continual process."

Learning as a Lifelong Commitment

More than 115 years ago, Salvation Army founder William Booth committed his organization to training its leaders not only in the classroom but in the field as well. One of Booth's earliest dictums stated:

We must teach them how to fight. . . . Let every one have a chance. God is no respecter of persons, nor sex either. . . . Every gift you need is here; they only want calling forth and cultivating and you will be fully provided for war. But, mind: you must train and teach and develop—NO PIPE-CLAY SOLDIERS will be of any service here—and establish your army in actual service. . . . They must learn as they fight and fight while they learn.

Tips for Establishing an Effective Training Program

We asked those involved in training programs at the Government Accounting Office, the Salvation Army, the Girl Scouts of the U.S.A., and Beth Israel Deaconess Medical Center to compile a list of what they regard as the essentials of an effective training program. Here is a composite of those lists:

- Make sure your training program includes courses, seminars, and informal sessions designed to educate everyone as to the mission and history of the organization.
- Include everyone in the training program, from receptionists and security guards to top management. Use the training program to make it clear that everyone in the organization is valued.
- If your organization utilizes volunteers, make certain that they are included in the training program. Treat them and their opinions as seriously as you do those of your paid workers.
- Make certain that top managers are highly visible at the training sessions and that their commitment to the program is apparent. Encourage interaction between those at the top and those from every level of the organization.

Tips for Establishing an Effective Training Program (continued)

- Use the training program as an opportunity to solicit feedback from staff and employees as to current issues, problems, and challenges within the organization.
- Based on the feedback you receive, design future training courses to address the issues, problems, and challenges that have been identified.
- Wherever possible, have your own staff and employees create and conduct the training courses.
- Make sure that a significant number of your training courses deal with issues that cross departmental lines. Make sure that representatives from all departments are involved in these courses.
- Include as many courses as you can that enable people to develop and enhance personal skills as well as skills related directly to their jobs.
- Make certain that all training courses are designed and conducted in a hands-on, participatory fashion. Divide participants into small groups to work on specific issues.
- Make certain that your training program places particular emphasis on the development of communications skills. Solicit feedback from participants as to what more needs to be done to make your organization one in which information and ideas are shared, people are listened to, and both the good and the bad news get out.
- Develop and conduct courses, seminars, and informal sessions that deal with the issue of diversity in the workforce.
- Make each of your training courses as practical as possible. Teach by example, not theory. Wherever possible, bring in people from other public-service organizations and from the private sector to discuss how they have dealt successfully with issues and challenges faced by your organization.
- Whenever possible, bring your customers into the training program. Give them the benefit of what your program has to offer and seize the opportunity to get feedback from them as to how you can serve them better.

Valuing People Means Helping Them Become Self-Reliant

No organization we encountered places more value on the people within its ranks than does the Delancey Street Foundation. That attitude is the key to Delancey Street's ability to turn former criminals and drug addicts into successful, self-reliant citizens and taxpayers. The success of the foundation stems from the fact that everyone earns his or her keep in one of the many businesses that support the program. Every one of its ventures serves as a training school as well as a profit-making operation. Each of Delancey Street's residents rotates through several of its businesses to pick up needed job skills. In addition to full-time vocational training, the program also includes training in interpersonal and communications skills as well as "school learning." All residents are tutored by other, more advanced residents until they earn a high school equivalency degree.

Because its mission is self-reliance, the easy way is not Delancey Street's way. At Delancey Street, the process of valuing people begins with the establishment of clear lines of individual accountability. This is an organization that bases its operations on four nos.

- No funding—government or foundation. Self-reliant people earn their own way.
- No staff. Self-reliance can't be learned by accepting help. It can only be learned by helping yourself.
- No excuses. Break the rules and accept the consequences. Screw up and learn to laugh at yourself—it's going to happen a lot.
- No time-outs. No retreats for healing before you get back in the game. Life is change, crisis is constant. Keep moving forward.

Above All, Valuing People Means Recognizing Their Contributions

Ask any group of public-service managers to list their five biggest challenges, and chances are that finding a substitute for the profit motive will appear high on every list. Everyone needs to be acknowledged for a job well done, and all of the effective organizations we visited place great emphasis on building systems of recognition and reward.

"You want to know my biggest management secret?" asks the National Theatre Workshop of the Handicapped's founder, Rick Curry. "I have a rule that every single week each staff member has to say something positive about another staff member in front of the student body. Why? It builds confidence in the students by showing them that as faculty we truly respect each other. And it's something that grows. When I say something nice about a certain faculty member, then he starts saying something positive about me and it's infectious." The entire organization has caught the founder/director's spirit, and all those affiliated with the NTWH are free with their praise. When their publicist lands a cover piece in a magazine or writes a great article, they let her know right away what a good job she's done. If one of the students writes a scene for a particular performance and they think it's terrific, everyone celebrates that success. The bottom line is, everybody at the NTWH realizes that the students take risks with everything they do and that positive reinforcement from staff and fellow students is essential.

Creating a Family Spirit

The U.S. Geological Survey (USGS) is one of the oldest of all federal agencies. It is renowned for the respect it shows all its employees, leading to a climate in which thirty-year service pins are not uncommon, fifty-year pins are not unique, and the agencywide turnover rate, including retirements and deaths, is only 5 percent a year. During our investigations, we discovered a prime example of the way the survey demonstrates the value it places on its people. In the early 1990s, there was a real threat of unpaid furloughs hanging over the heads of all federal employees. Almost all the government agencies decided that if this should come about, they would furlough their people beginning at the bottom of the organizational ladder. Not the USGS. Collectively, the organization decided that if one of its employees was required to go on unpaid furlough, then the entire agency would take unpaid furlough. When the survey's then director Dallas Peck heard about the plan, he insisted that he be included in it as well.

Develop Concrete Strategies to Reward Achievement

Peter Sterling, president of the Children's Museum of Indianapolis, carries a notebook around with him, in which he jots down every example of positive performance he sees. When he feels that his managers are not giving out enough awards for excellence, he cites the examples he has personally witnessed. "You have to continually make sure that people's worth is recognized," he says, "and in particular, you have to seek out and reward your champions." At the museum, time is set aside at every monthly staff meeting to swap stories of individual and group achievement. "It builds pride in everyone," says director of education David Cassady. "Even when it's orchestrated, it means a great deal to people." The shared stories of both large and small contributions inspire others at the museum to give more than 100 percent. At one meeting, for example, two museum secretaries were acknowledged for getting out an important grant application on time. When the office word processors broke down, the secretaries took the materials home three nights in a row and typed the lengthy applications on their own equipment.

The recognition of the worth and contributions of employees at every level has paid off in ways that have surprised even Peter Sterling. "We were struggling to come up with a plan to raise the money for our new building," he recalls. "The board of trustees was very skeptical and thought the plan too financially ambitious, especially the $25,000 we expected to raise in donations from employees. Well the employees gave $60,000, and it knocked the socks off the trustees, who then gave $1 million more than they were slated to contribute. Believe me, we made a point of collectively thanking all our family."

At New York's Department of Juvenile Justice (DJJ), developing reward strategies was one of the most important ingredients of former commissioner Ellen Schall's management approach. "We realized early on," says Schall, "that we couldn't get staff to care about kids until we demonstrated that we cared about the staff as well. And so we continually tried to find ways to appreciate staff's work, to celebrate every small win as it came along. It's very important not to wait until the end, because if you wait until the end to celebrate it just delays getting to the end." The DJJ held impromptu lunches and dinners whose sole purpose was to acknowledge staff achievements. Very few meetings took place without someone acknowledging someone else's efforts or accomplishments on a particular project.

Former commissioner Rose Washington cites a specific DJJ strategy to recognize innovation. "Soon after I became commissioner," she says, "I decided to organize a management staff of forty-five managers and department heads to meet every two months. In one of our early meetings, several people came up with great ideas, and it gave me an idea of my own. I went out and bought an enormous, inflatable light bulb. And now DJJ awards this 'idea bulb' to the person who comes up with the best idea. The bulb takes up a lot of room in an office, but believe me anyone who gets it makes sure it's on display."

One of the key elements in the turnaround of Webster Elementary School in Magna, Utah, was the Pride Program initiated by principal Cyndy Cannell. Any time a teacher saw something worth rewarding—from one student's holding the door for another to someone's picking up a piece of paper in the hall—that student was immediately given a pride ticket. Tickets were given out between classes, in assemblies, on the playground, and in the classroom.

Each week, the student who had amassed the most pride tickets received a reward that came in the form of a small gift: a dinner in a restaurant, a pizza, tickets to a movie—anything that showed appreciation. Everyone on the Webster staff—secretaries, social workers, maintenance personnel, kitchen staff—was empowered to give out pride tickets. The program proved so successful that it was emulated not only throughout the school district but in schools throughout the entire state of Utah as well.

We All Need Recognition

Dr. Mitch Rabkin relates an anecdote that reveals the importance of recognition to everyone in an organization, no matter what their level of position or sophistication. "When I was president of Boston's Beth Israel Hospital, we built a new wing in our main building," he explains. "There was a floor-to-ceiling display case installed in the lobby. We didn't quite know what to do with it. Then we decided that we'd put some kind of monthly exhibit inside the case. One of the first ideas we came up with called for a display of books written by Beth Israel authors. When the month was over, we started to remove the books and we nearly had a revolt on our hands engendered by doctors and nurses who were so proud of their literary achievements. Now that Beth Israel has merged with the Deaconess Hospital, that display case has become the home of a permanent exhibition of the current works of authors from both institutions. It is a real source of pride and inspiration, and no one dares replace it."

Nothing Beats Peer Recognition

One of the first ideas suggested in the Ochoco National Forest after the Forest Service chief and his top staff placed full operating power in the hands of forest personnel came from Tyler Groo, a technician and union steward. Groo suggested that every line person in the forest be granted the authority to give one award a year. The award was to be granted only by nonsupervisory personnel; no managers need apply. There was to be no approval criteria. Every nonsupervisor would get a certificate worth $25 that could be given to any deserving fellow employee for any good reason. The suggestion was adopted and named after its inventor.

Groo Awards have become highly coveted articles. "When I was in the private sector," states one Ochoco office supervisor, "I received several substantial cash rewards. But nothing has ever meant more to me than the three Groo Awards I have received from my colleagues." The awards were so effective from the start that, during the first year, forest supervisors began to clamor to give out their own Groos. Some supervisors even offered to turn in their official awards authority in return for being able to hand out Groo Awards. "It got so important to them," says the Ochoco's J. C. Hansen, "that in the second year, the employees said, 'okay, supervisors, you can have a Groo-type award, but it can't be a Groo Award because the Groo Awards are ours.'" The supervisors had to give in, and now there are Supervisory Groo Awards as well as the original Groos.

"Nothing," says the Ochoco's administrative officer, Rod Collins, "means more than recognition from co-workers. And we've learned something else from the award system. The first year the big winner was a quiet maintenance guy whom hardly anyone ever sees. Thanks to the Groos, we're discovering and rewarding people who would otherwise be overlooked."

The Groo Awards have proven so effective in boosting morale and recognizing real value that more than a hundred organizations have contacted Collins to find out how to have Groos of their own. These organizations include the Federal Aviation Administration in Oakland, California, the Environmental Protection Agency in Seattle, Washington, the U.S. Coast Guard, and private businesses like Ingersoll-Rand and Procter & Gamble.

Valuing Everyone

Director Mike Breslin and his staff at the Northumberland Children's Clinic found a special way of making the bureaucracy work for them. "The secret," says Breslin, "is to keep your eye on the customer and use the bureaucracy as a tool to get the job done. You have to view the rule enforcers as customers. They come in with their regulations and checklists and have a job to do. They're better paid than most of the people they regulate, but they are not happy where they are because they are nothing more than glorified rule enforcers. Most of them have real expertise and talent that is totally untouched and untapped. I encourage my staff to treat them like consultants—make them feel helpful, let them use their experience. It's amazing how, once they know how valued they are, they want to come here and be supportive and helpful."

No organization works well if people don't talk to one another. No organization truly succeeds if management remains aloof from staff and workers. Trust is lost if bad news is withheld. Much is gained if the good news is shared both inside and outside the organization. Establishing effective lines of communication is one the most difficult of all organization tasks. Yet, as we'll see in the next chapter, it *is* being done.

10

COMMUNICATING EFFECTIVELY

During the early stages of our project we placed hundreds of phone calls and sent an equal number of letters seeking general information and the opportunity to interview managers and employees of interesting organizations. Although we didn't fully realize it at the time, these first contacts had a real influence on our final selections. If our early inquiries went unheeded, if we were delayed or put off, we had immediate doubts about the overall quality of the organization, no matter how highly it had been recommended to us.

The same was true during our first visit to organizations we were considering. At one large government agency, for example, we got turned around in a maze of corridors and offices. Although we were obviously lost, not one of the several employees who passed by volunteered help or pointed us in the right direction. That negative first impression stayed with us, and, though it wasn't the only reason we decided not to include that agency, we couldn't help but be influenced by it.

All the public agencies and nonprofits we finally selected have this in common: They are friendly organizations full of friendly people who were interested in us and why we were interested in them. They introduced themselves and then went out of their way to introduce others. That's true also of the military facility and the federal prison we visited.

As we started to identify the traits and skills that characterize our organizations, we realized that this notion of friendliness isn't something we could prescribe. Friendliness is not a strategy; it's not something to learn and pass on. After many discussions, we finally concluded that what these friendly organizations do—something that could be learned—is communicate both often and well.

Employees are interested and involved in the work they do together, and they talk about it among themselves and with the outside world. These are organizations in which everyone, regardless of rank, function, or background, is encouraged to share his or her opinions freely, organizations where inevitable disputes are talked over and resolved openly.

We found it ironic that in this age of computers, satellites, fiber optics, and other high-tech advances, it is plain, old-fashioned, garden-variety, face-to-face talks that are the basis of strong communications. The U.S. Forest Service, for example, ties its far-flung operations together through a satellite network that gives everyone the opportunity to be in touch with everyone else. But what the Forest Service has discovered is that the sophisticated high-tech system is effective only when it works in tandem with face-to-face communications. Finally, we have learned that perhaps the greatest benefit of effective communication is its role as a great leveler or democratizer. Organizations with a rigid chain of command or hierarchy tend to cut off conversations and filter news. By encouraging full-scale, candid communication, the best nonprofits and government agencies, as you'll see in the following pages, create full-scale participation that goes a long way toward assuring top performance.

Communicate by Wandering Around

Tom Peters calls it "managing by wandering around." As Martha Baker, marketing director of the San Diego Zoo, says, "Here, managers learn on the street." Either way, an important part of communication is the vital strategy of leaving the isolation of the office and joining the action. It is communication without agenda, and it happens on the run. The results are unpredictable, but the odds of discovering something exciting are good. Most important, by wandering around a manager communicates concern for everything that is going on.

During our visits to the San Diego Zoo, we rarely had the chance to sit down. As soon as we began to inquire about a particular project, someone would get up and say, "Let's go check it out." We started one of our tours in the company of executive director Douglas Myers and the zoo's general manager Art Risser. But this official excursion soon changed into a working one. When we visited a construction site, Myers and Risser stopped to consult with workers on some equipment damage. Along the way, they greeted every employee we met. They stopped for a dozen small, informal conferences with workers, and they paused to visit almost every animal, noting a new arrival here or the need for a hoof trim there. They were constantly aware of the visitors around them, asking them what their experiences were. If they thought we were in the way, they moved us to another spot so that visitors could have the best access to the exhibits. Along the way, they noticed cleaners who were behind schedule and made a note to find out why. Once Risser stopped to pick up trash, probably the only piece we saw in two days. All this in one forty-minute stroll. It was obvious to us that Risser and Myers were having fun. That is an important part of the message they convey to employees. Imagine how powerful that message would be in a machine-tool factory or a school—the notion that top management can't resist spending time on the line because it is so much fun. What would that do for morale? Most important, Risser and Myers were working as well. They could follow the progress of construction through memos or read about their customers in surveys, but instead of learning through the in-basket, they learn on the street.

Honesty Is the Only Policy

Unless you share all the news—good and bad—whatever you're communicating is just propaganda. The only solid foundation for fostering full participation is full and free sharing of information. In 1985, Captain Bill Lloyd, commanding officer of the Alameda Naval Aviation Depot, instituted a quarterly briefing or walkaround, a tradition that his successors, Captain Bill Tinston and Captain R. W. Smith, carried on. Every ninety days "the Skipper" visited sites around the huge base, where he made a presentation to employees, bringing them up to date on the state of the business, where they stood on performance targets, projected workloads for the coming quarter, and other matters. Good news or bad news, it was all shared. Then the Skipper took questions. The questions and the captain's responses were published in an employee information sheet.

Alameda's policy of sharing all the news served it in good stead during several periods of crisis faced by all military facilities. Like many other bases and depots, Alameda appeared several times on the Department of Defense's list of potential base closings before it finally was shut down in June 1996. During these periods, the full disclosure of good news and bad to all employees helped to stop the flow of rumors and keep all workers focused on the tasks at hand.

Don't Stand on Ceremony

Hierarchies tend to filter out bad news as it climbs higher through the organization. That was not the case at the Baltimore County Police Department under Chief Neil Behan. "I suspect," says the former chief, "that American organizations may be among the worst communicators in the world. In the Baltimore County Police Department, in addition to the chain of command, I set up as many levels of communication as I could—with my supervisors, with the officers, with the union. I had a liaison officer on my staff, a regular cop—no rank, no threat—and anybody could come to him and get right to me."

Behan's emphasis on communication paid off when the department was establishing its COPE units. As happens with most new projects, the program had its share of critics. Some saw community policing as a public-relations gimmick. Others viewed it simply as a ploy to placate the county's citizens. There was strong opposition within the police department itself. "There will always be members of the force," says one officer, "who feel that the officers at COPE are not doing real police work."

In order to combat criticism, Behan and his commanders launched an intensive campaign to communicate the value of the COPE program to the entire police force. "I personally conducted training sessions designed to make all our people aware of COPE's purpose," says Behan. "We had the new COPE officers visit every station house and explain the program and its benefits to the whole force as well as to the community. We conducted regular workshops at which we brought in experts. We targeted these workshops both at COPE officers and officers from other departments. Most important, we listened to every bit of criticism and addressed everyone's concerns openly, both in formal meeting and around the water cooler and in the squad room. We're proud of what COPE is accomplishing, but we would never have gotten off the ground if we had not communicated the purposes, the goals, and the workings of the program to everyone."

COPE's Formula for Successful Communications

Focus on customers' perceptions.   Focus on developing an advocacy relationship with those you serve.

Research, analyze, substantiate, and communicate customers' perceptions of problems.   Conduct door-to-door interviews. Administer surveys. Consult experts from the academic community and the private sector. Conduct community meetings.

Develop and implement short-range and long-range solutions.   Hold brainstorming sessions. Involve all levels of staff. Write plans of action.

Maintain dialogue.   Explore all avenues for developing ways to work cooperatively to solve customer problems. Anticipate future problems and develop plans for addressing them. Communicate continually with everyone.

You Cannot Overcommunicate

Large, complex, decentralized organizations fight entropy with constant, open-ended, formal and informal communications. A major medical facility, like Boston's Beth Israel Deaconess Medical Center, for instance, is made up of dozens of divisions and disciplines. In most hospitals, each function is isolated. People in the pharmacy or the laboratory or other departments tend to live in their own worlds. Not so at Beth Israel Deaconess, where staff members constantly talk with one another. "Working in a lab," says one medical technologist, "I have a direct effect on patient care. There are times when we are the first to recognize problems and notify the physicians. I think a big part of all our success is our ability to communicate." Says a clinical pharmacist, "Beth Israel Deaconess's pharmacy department is clinically oriented. I attend pharmacy rounds with medical teams to monitor how certain patients are doing. I interact with doctors and nurses on a regular basis."

Communicating well doesn't automatically assure that everything will go smoothly. The process of working and talking together inevitably leads to disagreements. At Beth Israel Deaconess, employees know that when two of them disagree, they can go to their boss together. It is an organizational policy, and the medical center's managers are trained to handle disputes. Employees know that both sides of an issue will be heard and that a solution will be found based on respect for each person's opinion. By bringing disputes out into the open and by arriving at decisions jointly, employees are engaging in win-win, rather than win-lose, situations.

This passion for communicating is carried over into print. The scope and frequency of their publications rival those of a small publishing house. "It is important to communicate to all our staff and employees about everything that goes on in this medical center and about the medical profession in general," says Dr. Mitch Rabkin, CEO of Caregroup, Inc., the medical center's parent organization. "We publish newsletters targeted to the doctors, the employees, the trustees, the patients. We print them in Spanish, Haitian, and French as well as in English." The medical center also publishes a magazine featuring articles on every area of health care, catalogues describing the various opportunities for training at the hospital, employee handbooks, and detailed booklets containing information for patients. Monthly financial reports are distributed to every employee. Beth Israel Deaconess also uses AlertLine to circulate upcoming and recent news stories about the medical center and selected articles about advances in health care.

Actions Speak Louder Than Words

Dr. Mitch Rabkin is fond of telling the story about the Beth Israel Hospital board member, a successful elderly businessman, who came to the hospital one day soon after Rabkin was appointed its president and suggested that they take a walk through the corridors together. They went up to the fourth floor and strolled down the corridor. "Why are there papers on the floor?" the trustee asked the new chief executive. "I guess it's because no one has picked them up," replied Rabkin. The trustee then suggested an experiment: "Let's you and I pick up half of the papers on this floor and then go up to the sixth floor, stroll down the corridor where everyone can see us, but let's leave the papers on that floor untouched. We'll come back in a few minutes and check both corridors." When they rechecked both floors, the fourth-floor corridor was spotless while the papers on the sixth floor remained untouched. The trustee said, "It's not because people won't pick them up. It's because *you* won't—if you're so fancy you can't stoop down to pick up a bit of litter, why should they?" "What did I learn?" asks Rabkin. "When, as a leader, you ignore something, others will follow your lead."

Constant Communication with Customers Is Critical

The success of Seattle, Washington, in establishing its effective recycling program can be credited to the constant communication between the Solid Waste Utility (SWU) and its customers. For instance, when the SWU launched a new curbside pickup program, it sent out customer comment cards and received 110,000 responses out of 230,000 mailings. The utility also got numerous telephone responses, so many, in fact, that according to then director of customer service and finance John Anthony, "We literally blew out the city's phone system with over 35,000 calls." In the private sector, this kind of customer reaction probably would have motivated a company to delegate the task of answering the calls to a battery of temporary employees. Operating on a very limited budget, however, Anthony had to find staff volunteers who would answer calls in addition to doing their own work. Proudly displayed on his wall was the John "Just One More Call" Anthony Award for Customer Service, awarded to him for all the times he prowled the halls, stopping people and saying, "Just come on in here and answer the calls for two minutes, just two minutes."

Those involved in the Rochester School District's reform efforts knew from the beginning that none of their programs or approaches could succeed without the support and participation of the district's parents. This led to the establishment of the Home Base Guidance Program, through which each student is assigned to a teacher-adviser who serves as the student's advocate during the middle school years. The teacher/advisers establish and maintain a direct line of communication between the home and the school and among subject teachers. Before the beginning of each school year, advisers meet with incoming students and their parents. They get to know each other, and they discuss school and home expectations. Throughout the school year, advisers, through in-school conferences, telephone calls, and home visits, maintain close lines of communication with the parents. They work together to help motivate students in their school work, to encourage them to participate in extracurricular activities, and to promote attendance.

In its determination to involve parents in every way possible, the district has also supported and worked closely with the Union of Parents (UP), an advocacy group funded through the Rochester New Futures Initiative and administered by the Center for Educational Development. The UP recognizes that parents have both the right and the responsibility to be involved in decisions that affect their child's development and works to link individual parents, parent groups, schools, and community agencies to share information and to bring about positive change. It is also designed as a vehicle to provide technical assistance to strengthen existing school-parent groups and to organize such groups where none exist. Says the UP's organizer, Shirley Thompson, "The systemic change that this school system is attempting will succeed only if there is this type of parental involvement and only if parents and the schools are constantly in communication with one another. As customers we need to continually define and express our wishes, and the schools need to communicate their responses to our ideas in a timely manner."

My Dog Ate My Homework

The Rochester School District's Monroe Middle School has come up with an innovative way to aid parents when they are confronted with a child's age-old fabrication, "Really Mom, I don't have any homework." The school has installed homework phone lines, open twenty-four hours a day, upon which each teacher leaves a three-minute message informing parents what homework they have assigned for that day or week. Though many students undoubtedly wish it had never been installed, it's a communications strategy that is proving highly effective.

Don't Hesitate to Blow Your Own Horn

Few public-service organizations put much emphasis on solid public relations as an important aspect of communicating with customers. We're not advocating overselling an organization's achievements. But top-performing organizations, especially nonprofits and public agencies, cannot afford to let their stakeholders remain ignorant of their accomplishments.

Sandra J. Hale took on her new job as head of Minnesota's Department of Administration knowing that government had a reputation for being slow, wasteful, and poorly managed. She knew also that her agency was reputed to be one of the most bureaucratic. But she began to find out that these perceptions were far from the truth. "I began to realize," she says, "that for every example of waste and mismanagement, I could find ten examples of dedicated, superior performance and innovative thinking." She had found her mission—exposing good government. Throughout the time she was in office she carried out this mission by constantly spreading the message of competence throughout the state.

"The biggest problem in getting the good news out," says Hale, "is that the press is not quick to cover positive achievements. Also, there is the fact that there are reporters who cover politics and reporters who cover business, but there are few who cover the business of government, so it's hard to get noticed when you're doing a good job."

Hale overcame this obstacle by actively seeking out media coverage for her programs and achievements. She held regular press conferences and wrote numerous articles on her agency's accomplishments and submitted them to newspapers, magazines, and journals throughout the country. "Positive press," says Hale, "not only boosts employees' morale, but it's like money in the bank that can be used when the inevitable hard times arrive."

Beth Israel Deaconess Medical Center's passion for communicating, for example, doesn't stop at the front door. "In an institution as dynamic as ours," says Dr. Mitch Rabkin, "events, achievements, and changes take place with some frequency. Many developments are of interest to the public or a segment of the public. Some are particularly important to the hospital's task of shaping its public perception with the taste, accuracy, and judiciousness so important when hospitals and doctors are increasingly under the shadow of judgments that can be harsh and publicity that can be adverse." Beth Israel Deaconess's many publications aimed at the general public are designed to present a positive image of the medical center in particular and the medical profession in general by describing the range of quality services and the scope of medical advances that this one institution provides. Beth Israel Deaconess's doctors, nurses, and other staff add to this positive literature through the many books and articles they write. The medical center's nurses have averaged more than thirty publications a year. In addition, they communicate the advances they've made in their profession in general and to the medical center in particular by making more than 120 presentations annually throughout the United States and abroad.

Conduct a Constant Review of the Effectiveness of Your Communications Strategies

The U.S. Forest Service, staffed by 40,000 employees spread throughout the nation, has always prided itself on its understanding of the importance of effective communications within the organization. The Forest Service was one of the first public agencies to provide every one of its employees with a computer and to create a network through which all employees could communicate with each other and with the Washington office. It was also among the first government agencies to use the latest technologies such as video teleconferencing. In addition, the agency committed itself to the production and distribution of brochures and videos and the use of direct mail to communicate the many management initiatives emanating from the chief and staff in the Washington office.

In 1992, based on feedback from the field, deputy chief for administration Lamar Beasley commissioned a major internal study involving seventeen field sites located throughout the United States to determine how well management was communicating with the field, particularly regarding the agency's management initiatives. After interviewing dozens of employees at each of the seventeen sites, the study team, headed by consultant Carol Weiss, concluded that management was flooding the system with far too many management initiatives. The staff simply could not determine which initiatives were most important and which required the most immediate attention, especially since there often was no strategic context accompanying the initiative, and expectations were often either unstated or unclear. The findings also revealed that frequently there was too long an interval between the announcement of an initiative and its arrival in the field. Added to all of this were employees' complaints about their lack of participation in the creation of the initiatives and their lack of adequate opportunity to provide feedback once an initiative was instituted.

Based on these findings, the study team then issued a set of specific recommendations designed to remedy the ways in which management initiatives were communicated and to establish standards by which the Forest Service could become a model of excellence in communication. These recommendations included:

- Set priorities. There is simply too much "stuff" out there, along with too many mixed messages and competing objectives. Most organizations are not able to invest in and effectively implement more than two or three major change initiatives in any one given period.
- Each year, select two or three of the most important management initiatives. Communicate these initiatives clearly, concisely, and with one voice.
- Put initiative into an organizational context, stating clearly how it relates to other initiatives and priorities.
- Make certain that the initiative addresses such practical matters as how it will change the way business is done, how it will affect specific locations, and how it will affect all individuals involved.
- Identify the key stakeholders who will be affected by the initiative and then decide on what will be the most effective way to communicate with them. Consider asking such questions as: Who is the target audience? What do they need to know in order to implement this initiative? Are there similar initiatives floating around? What else is going on in the organization at this time that can help or hinder the understanding and implementing of this initiative? Who can best "champion" the initiative? What do we expect people to do based on this initiative? What kind of followup and feedback are planned around this initiative? How can we reinforce this initiative? How will we know if the communication has been received by the target audience? How will we know if the initiative has been implemented?
- Decide which existing initiatives can be "weeded out."
- Develop yardsticks to determine if initiatives have been implemented throughout the organization.
- Develop the management initiatives in a participatory manner.
- Discuss and build consensus around each initiative with top executives, staff, and key personnel from the field. Agree on goals, objectives, actions, target dates, and desired results.
- Involve people from every level of the organization in the conceptualization and creation of the initiative.
- Set clear expectations and develop a strategy and timelines for communicating the initiative throughout the agency.

- Follow up and monitor the progress of the communication and implementation of the initiative with those in the field.
- Set dates for feedback on how the initiative is being implemented, and communicate this to the rest of the organization.
- Explain, emphasize, and promote the initiative throughout the agency to the overseers, to the public, and to all key stakeholders.
- Consider making major changes in the format and distribution of the initiative.
- Relying on a slick brochure as a primary means of presenting an initiative internally is not effective. Emphasis should be placed on presenting the initiatives in an easy to read, simple format. This, along with brevity and a reduction in the number of initiatives, will go a long way toward assuring that the initiatives are read and remembered.
- Forums should be established in the field so that management can introduce an initiative personally and employees can have the opportunity to air their concerns and submit their suggestions.

Dare to Discuss the Tough Issues

The Forest Service has been working to implement these communication strategies under the aegis of the Clinton administration's Reinventing Government Initiative. Encouraged by its parent agency, the Department of Agriculture, the Forest Service's reinvention team has focused on enhancing its communications skills and efforts.

In a series of "town hall" meetings in eight selected sites throughout the nation the Forest Service opened communication with special interests and community groups. Approximately four hundred people were invited to each meeting through letters that informed them that "the Forest Service is looking at all areas of the agency in its approach to reinventing itself." The public was asked to provide new ideas and concepts to address the following five areas:

Purpose
What should we be?
   Is the century-old mission of the agency aligned with today's knowledge and needs?

Culture
Who should we be?
   Are our traditional beliefs, values, norms, and behaviors adequate to address tomorrow's concerns? Are we the appropriate work force for the 21st century? What work force

and leadership attributes are appropriate for the 21ˢᵗ century Forest Service?

Work
How should we do it?

How can we improve our customer service? How can we make more effective our method of doing things?

Outcomes
What can we provide you?

What products and services would you like us to provide?

Structure
How should we be organized?

On an ecosystem basis? On a state-by-state basis? What should our organizational profile look like?

In order to ensure that communication during the meetings was as meaningful and as effective as possible, strict ground rules were established:

Introduction (5 minutes).   Forest Service Chief Thomas, Assistant Secretary Lyons, and other officials welcomed all the participants and spoke briefly about the goals of the reinvention team.

Overview of the Meeting (10 minutes).   A Forest Service official explained the goals of the meeting, describing how participants would be broken into small groups of eight to ten people for discussion and how the discussion would be facilitated by a person chosen to be moderator and written down in note form by another individual selected as recorder/spokesperson.

Group Discussion (50 minutes).   Each person in the group was given the opportunity to express his or her opinion. Group members were invited to clarify an idea but not debate it. After the discussion, the reporter/spokesperson read back his or her notes and gave a two- to three-minute synthesis of the ideas that people felt most strongly about and that would be shared with the larger group. The recorder/spokesperson was reminded that he or she was to report the feelings of the whole group, not a personal point of view.

Group Reports (45 minutes).   Recorder/spokespeople from each group gave their reports. At all eight initial town hall meetings, only two spokespeople attempted to represent their own points of view after they had given the group report. In each case they were shouted down by the assembly.

Feedback (10 minutes).   After the group reports were concluded, the chief and other officials provided feedback to the entire group on what they had heard and put this information into a larger context wherever possible. They also commented briefly on other ideas that had emerged from other town hall meetings.

Closing.   All participants were invited to remain and hold informal discussions with the chief and other officials. During the group reports and feedback sessions, a capsule summary of all ideas presented was compiled by computer, and this summary was handed out to all participants. All members of the group were informed that they would be sent a fuller synopsis of the meeting along with the names of Forest Service officials in their region with whom they could follow up by exchanging additional ideas.

From its inception, the Forest Service reinvention team has adopted as its motto the slogan, "What if we could just start over?" The town hall meetings have gone a long way toward helping the agency reinvent itself. In the process, it has reaped a most important additional benefit—the honing of its communications skills.

Making a Town Hall Meeting Work

U.S. Forest Service and Department of Agriculture officials feel strongly that the town hall meeting concept is one from which all organizations can benefit. They are quick to point out, however, that the tight guidelines utilized in their town hall meetings are essential to the success of those meetings. Following are tips that these officials have provided for making the roles of the moderator and the recorder/spokesperson as effective as possible:

The Moderator

- Pass around the sign-in sheets. Make sure everyone signs in. Be sure to collect the sheets before the group disbands.
- Have each member of your discussion group introduce him/herself.
- Ensure that you appoint a recorder/spokesperson from within the group.
- Make sure each person in your group is given a fair chance to express his/her opinions—even if others disagree.
- Allow disagreement but not a long debate. (A consensus is not required.)
- Do not monopolize the discussion, facilitate it.
- Stop discussion at the appropriate time.
- At the conclusion of the discussion group, coordinate a discussion review between your group and the recorder/spokesperson.
- At the end of the meeting, collect the written notes from the recorder/spokesperson.

The Recorder/Spokesperson

- Please make sure your notes are legible.
- Take notes of the basic points only.
- Quantify or weigh your notes (*all . . . most . . . some said*).
- After discussion, review your notes with the group.

◆▸

Making a Town Hall Meeting Work (continued)

- Check legibility of your notes and provide the Moderator with your notes before leaving the meeting.
- Include your name, address, and phone number on your notes.
- Orally summarize at least the main points from your group (those ideas about which most group members felt strongly).
- Represent the group, not yourself, in your oral summary.
- Keep your summary within the agreed-upon time frame.

Fundamentals of Effective Communicating

We asked Dr. Mitch Rabkin of Beth Israel Deaconess to summarize what he sees as the fundamentals of effective communicating. Here is his list:

- Effective communication has to start at the top. Leaders must clearly articulate their vision and their goals and must make certain that everyone at every level is aware of them.
- A climate must be created in which everyone at every level truly listens to everyone else. Free exchanges of ideas and opinions must be constantly encouraged. Everyone's ideas and opinions must be treated with respect.
- Managers must be responsible for sharing all the news concerning the organization—good and bad—up and down the line.
- Lines of communication must be established not only internally but with customers and the public at large. Customers must constantly be made aware of new approaches and new programs. News of achievements should be shared with the public.

CONCLUSION
Putting It All Together

Tell them what you are going to do. Do it. Summarize what you've done." Somewhere along the line, almost all of us have encountered this time-honored formula for effectively putting forth detailed information. In our introduction, we laid out what we intended to do in this book. We hope we've delivered as promised. Here's where we summarize, where we pull together as succinctly as we can, the basic approaches and hottest strategies that emerged from our journey into the public and nonprofit sectors. We think this summary a helpful device that will enable you to quickly review the strategies that most caught your attention, those that you feel will be most beneficial to you and/or your organization.

Begin with Mission

Government and nonprofit organizations begin with mission. All of our organizations recognize that their mission is the unifying and the single irreplaceable element in their makeup.

Define your mission. Put it out there for all to see.

Every project undertaken by the Girl Scouts is measured by its potential benefits "for the girls." At the San Diego Zoo, even sales clerks in the gift shop can tell their customers how each item in the shop is part of the zoo's mission of conservation and preservation.

Don't dabble. Stick to your mission. . . .	The Nature Conservancy is constantly asked to join forces with other environmental groups in lawsuits or special-issue campaigns. They resist temptation and give their full attention to the mission of preserving the endangered natural world.
. . . But there are exceptions.	Twice in the last decade, to meet the changing needs of their customers, New York City's Department of Juvenile Justice has expanded its mission.
If expansion of the mission is deemed necessary, get everyone involved.	DJJ's successful expansions of mission have been made possible by the way in which the agency has approached each expansion deliberately through small starts and by making sure that consensus for each expansion is reached at every level of the organization.
Use the mission as a recruiting tool.	The Government Accounting Office competes with the private sector for recruits. It compensates for its inability to pay top salaries by constantly emphasizing the challenges, the importance, and the psychic rewards connected with the work it performs.

Embrace Change

Although complacency is a label often hung on public and nonprofit organizations, all of the agencies we cite are committed to constant change. They don't try to hide behind rules, regulations, and bureaucracies. They embrace change. They see it as a fact of life. They identify innovative, ingenious, even disruptive employees and make them champions. They initiate lots of small starts and pilot programs.

Change begins with customers.	The Girl Scouts rebounded from a significant drop in membership by hanging to meet the

changing needs of the girls. Armed with data from their biennial surveys, they've started programs for younger girls, programs in housing projects, programs for the homeless, programs for girls with incarcerated mothers, and programs for girls from a rainbow of ethnic backgrounds.

Give your change champions the power they need to be effective.

The magic of the STEP program of Minnesota's Department of Administration was that it put the power to change in the hands of anyone who was motivated to make it. STEP had no resources or bureaucratic power, just support for people who were ready to change.

Be sure to listen to champions who challenge you.

Tyler Groo is a forestry technician in the Ochoco National Forest. Groo is a man who knows his own mind and speaks it without regard for how his message will be received. (Rod Collins, the administrative chief of the forest, calls Groo "the Socrates of the Ochoco.") In fact, for many years, Groo has worked nine months of the year for the Forest Service and the other three months on his own time, working in the forest doing the jobs he felt needed to be done and that the Forest Service was not willing to fund. Groo's suggestions and innovations may be impolitic at times, but they have fueled many of the Ochoco's change initiatives.

Don't be afraid to act quickly.

At the Delancey Street Foundation, the fundamental philosophy is constant change. And the foundation lives its philosophy. If someone in this self-supporting agency comes up with a good business or a program idea, that person will get to work exploring the possibility immediately, working late into the night.

The foundation of change is small starts.	The systemic reform of the Rochester public schools began with a series of pilot programs at the elementary school level. These enabled school officials to evaluate and recalibrate before launching extensive change. The early pilots demonstrated success and built confidence and esprit de corps.
Mistakes are inevitable. Learn from them.	Those involved in the Rochester school reform movement are quick to admit that, in their attempt to affect change in every facet of the way the district's schools are run, they have made many mistakes. They admit these mistakes openly, view them as learning experiences, and focus on correcting them.
Look over your shoulder; they may be gaining on you.	The Children's Museum of Indianapolis is a world leader in its field. To stay on top, management and employees continually explore new strategies and new ideas.
Practice creative "swiping."	Staff and employees at the Indianapolis museum constantly visit other museums to see what is new and effective at these places. They are never reluctant to take an idea that works and make it their own.

Manage for Results

What gets measured, gets done. This maxim is true for every organization—public and private, profit or nonprofit. Every organization that delivers outstanding service does it by setting clear and measurable performance standards and then measuring performance.

Begin with planning. Then get right down to work.

Under commissioners Ellen Schall and Rose Washington, New York City's Department of Juvenile Justice became an organization that plans, plans, plans. It broke down its complex mission into manageable chunks and set clear, step-by-step objectives to advance toward its goals. But as important as planning is, the DJJ never fell in love with planning for its own sake. Planning is the foundation for a focus on measurable results. And—make no mistake—results are what this organization is about.

Make change by setting—and meeting—long- and short-term goals.

The Seattle Solid Waste Utility has become the most successful agency of its kind in the nation, due in great measure to the fact that it set and met ambitious long-term goals of reducing solid waste by 40 percent. Ambitious goals inspire awesome performance. But the longest journey is made step by step, and the Solid Waste Utility also paid careful attention to setting short-term objectives, measuring effectiveness, taking compass readings, and making frequent course corrections.

No one system is best for everyone.

The U.S. Geological Survey knows that one size doesn't fit all. Each of its four traditional program divisions has unique missions and performance standards. The National Mapping Division, because of its tangible products, is managed very much like a private corporation, complete with marketing experts and a sales force. The Geologic Division maintains its effectiveness by constantly having field staff swap places with staff at national headquarters. The Water Resources Division is managed collaboratively with local government agencies throughout the nation. The Biological Resources Division is so relatively new, that a particular management style has not been put into place. Typical of the way USGS operates, several management approaches will be tried in order to determine which is most effective for this particular division.

Hold everyone accountable.

The Salvation Army operates with a series of checks and balances unrivaled in either the public or private sectors. Every officer, employee, and volunteer is under constant review. Local units are required to submit plans and results regularly to regional offices, which in turn must submit their plans and results to national headquarters. Officers and employees whose performance falls short are transferred to lesser jobs.

Measure, measure, measure.

The city of Phoenix, Arizona, measures the performance of each city department based, in part, on customer surveys. (These customer ratings are factored in when determining department heads' salaries.) The city also publishes the results of a biennial customer survey— hard numbers compiled by an independent marketing firm.

Serve the Customer

All these organizations exist first and foremost for their customers. They know their customers, live for them, and are insatiably curious about them. They spend as much time as possible with customers, even bringing them into agency operations. And that's just the basic stuff. These organizations go well beyond the basics, serving customers with different—even contradictory—preferences and priorities.

Every contact is critical; every customer is special.

If you can't make customer contact positive, you should at least make it less negative. Carlos Arauz, the city of Phoenix's personnel director, points out that most citizen contacts with government are negative. No one likes paying a ticket or a water bill. When Phoenix's citizens apply for a city job, Arauz and his people focus on making sure that disappointed candidates are treated with courtesy and dispatch.

The officers who served in Baltimore County's COPE police force units understood that, historically, most citizen encounters with police have been negative. Their job was to keep in close contact with citizens and to act as advocates for them.

When a new exhibit or facility opens at the San Diego Zoo, there's something special for each group of customers, from the board of directors and million-dollar donors to the newest family member. The zoo's staff makes sure that each group is recognized for its contribution.

Customer service demands heart.

Principal Cyndy Cannell led an amazing turnaround of Webster Elementary School in Magna, Utah. Her tactics and strategies were impeccable. Her results were astounding. It was all built on her passion for education, her love for students and teachers—in short, her heart.

Compassion is an essential ingredient in the way that the Phoenix fire department operates. Once a citizens is sent to the hospital in a fire department ambulance, paramedics at the scene make sure that anything in the citizen's house or apartment that has been disrupted is put back in place.

It takes guts, too.

The National Theatre Workshop of the Handicapped is all guts. Providing professional theatrical training for the disabled is not an easy sell, but they do it day in, day out.

Baltimore County's community policing program had to fight resistance from its own officers to provide the new COPE service for citizens. But it stayed with the program and served as an early model for police departments around the nation.

Customer service begins with knowing who your customers are.

The city of Phoenix and the Girl Scouts keep in touch with their customers by surveys and by following approval ratings and demographic trends closely.

The Children's Museum of Indianapolis keeps in touch by bringing its young customers in not just as paying visitors, but as board members and even exhibit designers.

The COPE units of the Baltimore County police force spent most of their time in the community ferreting out citizens' concerns regarding crime. Their greatest discovery was the fact that citizens' concerns were often very different from those imagined by the police department.

Everyone must participate.

Beth Israel Deaconess Medical Center trains *everyone*, from parking lot attendants to physicians, in customer service. Everyone is expected to meet customers and to help them. The same is true at the San Diego Zoo.

Customer-driven organizations put people before programs.

The Children's Clinic of Pennsylvania's Northumberland County combats bureaucratic barriers by bringing clients and their families together with representatives of all the county's service agencies. No one leaves the table until a workable program has been mapped out.

Quality is focused on customer needs.

The landing-gear quality group at the Alameda Naval Air Station virtually eliminated waste and error and improved turnaround in maintaining this vital component of the aircraft. The payoff was clear on the bottom line. Although members of the group were proud of their efforts in improving base performance, their efforts were also focused on quality for the sake of pilot safety.

Customer-driven organizations are of the customer, by the customer, and for the customer.

Look at Delancey Street. This foundation has a permanent staff of one and a customer population of more than one thousand in four sites around the country. The inmates are running the institution! And they're doing a better job than the professionals.

Customer-driven organizations bring customers *inside*.

At the Children's Museum of Indianapolis, they say the apostrophe indicates ownership. Children don't just enjoy the museum, they help the grownups design it. And you'll find their signatures on the back of every exhibit to which they contribute.

Share the Power

The organizations in this book have reversed the normal polarities, pushing power out of the executive suites and down toward the front line. When staff are put in charge of their own world, they work harder and more effectively. When decisions can be made on the line—where organizations are closest to customers—organizations can move faster and more flexibly to meet the challenges of change.

Get the power out of the executive suite and away from headquarters.	At the Alameda Naval Aviation Depot, each department head and foreman was a designated CEO with the power to run his or her operation as a small business. As a result, costs went down, performance went up, and quality rose dramatically.
Power sharing starts at the top.	It makes sense. Power sharing has to start with the guy who has power to share. The pilot program in the U.S. Forest Service's Ochoco Forest gave those in the forest the power to make some bold innovations. The men and women in the Ochoco were free to be bold because the chief of the Forest Service let it be known from the beginning that when mistakes were made, he would "take the heat."
Share *real* power.	The Children's Museum of Indianapolis lets children help design programs and exhibits—and follows their suggestions, even when it hurts.
	The Salvation Army's programs are planned and executed at the local level with input from the community. Local officers get to shape their own programs, but they have to find the money to support them.
	Boston's Beth Israel Hospital led the field in turning the real power for managing patient care over to nurses.

The Nature Conservancy puts the major responsibility and authority for carrying out its mission into the hands of those closest to the action. Its state chapters are responsible for identifying land that supports endangered plants and animals and, in most cases, they are given the authority to do what it takes to purchase the land and save it from development.

Power sharing pays off even in high-risk situations.

The Baltimore County Police Department let its COPE patrol officers set their own schedules, determine priorities, and make their own decisions.

Sharing power with teams increases involvement and creativity and reduces risk.

The Rochester, New York, school reform movement (like others around the country) puts management in the hands of school-based teams made up of teachers, administrators, parents, community representatives, and even students.

The San Diego Zoo has restructured itself. Its exhibits are managed by interdisciplinary teams that coordinate everything from animal care to customer service. The zoo also puts teams in charge of special projects such as finding ways to reduce water use.

Share power to defuse turf issues.

The Northumberland County, Pennsylvania, Children's Clinic brings together staff from every level of relevant county agencies to provide services for children in need. Everyone works together for the customer. They don't fight over turf or budgets or labels on a case file.

Value People

The organizations in this book treat every employee with respect. Whether employees are full-time or part-time, paid or volunteer, these organizations recognize and reward them, train them, and honor them for their spirit and achievements.

Treat people with trust and respect.

At Webster Elementary, respect meant courtesy and consideration for privacy. When an outbreak of head lice occurred at the school, the principal personally inspected every child's hair so that no one would know who had lice and who didn't.

Training is a centerpiece of valuing people.

Training is an investment in human capital. It is an indication of the organization's commitment to its people. Training at the Government Accounting Office is designed by the agency's managers. The training center is located on the same floor as the top executive offices.

Beth Israel Deaconess Medical Center provides training in hundreds of areas, including job skills and life skills.

Through its two national training centers, the Girl Scouts of the U.S.A. provides its staff and paid and unpaid workers with one of the most comprehensive and high-powered training programs in the nation. Training program officials make certain that each trainee selects courses that will directly enhance her job performance and personal growth as well as benefiting the organization as a whole.

Don't leave people in the lurch.

After seven years as commissioner of New York's Department of Juvenile Justice, Ellen Schall decided to leave her post. She announced her intention and then worked with her staff to plan for a successor. Eventually, they were able to bring in one of their own to replace Schall.

Recognize and reward people; it fuels the fires of performance.

The director of the Children's Museum of Indianapolis demands that all managers regularly recognize those who contribute positively to the organization. He carries around a notebook in which he lists achievements or good deeds that he spots.

Sandra Stiner Lowe, the driving force behind Fairfax County's Medical Care for Children Project, writes thank-you notes every day to honor employees and partners.

The head of the National Theatre Workshop of the Handicapped has a rule. At every student assembly, each member of the staff is required to praise a fellow staff member for something he or she has accomplished.

Don't let recognition be routine. Be imaginative.

Rose Washington, former head of the New York City Department of Juvenile Justice, gave a giant light-bulb-shaped balloon to the creator of the brightest idea of the month.

At the Webster Elementary School, staff and teachers gave out "pride cards" to students whom they "caught" doing something positive.

The best recognition comes from peers.

At the Ochoco National Forest, every nonsupervisor gives out Groo Awards. This award can be given to any colleague for any reason. The awards have become highly coveted, and recipients display them proudly.

Create a Climate for Innovation

In this world of constant change, every organization has been forced to find new ways of doing things. Effective organizations solicit new ideas from everyone. They listen to each idea and act quickly upon those that make sense. They recognize and reward innovators and contributors for ideas that work. They encourage everyone to examine other organizations for good ideas to "swipe." Most important, they make innovation a hallmark of everything they do, from reducing costs and increasing resources to serving their customers.

Don't dismiss any new idea.	At one of the Medical Care for Children Project's fundraising meetings, someone suggested holding a golf tournament. The response was, "Not again; I'd pay not to have to participate in another golf tournament." So the project held a Phantom Golf Tournament; people paid for the privilege of not having to show up. It raised thousands of dollars and has become an annual event.
Be imaginative.	When Cyndy Cannell was principal of Webster Elementary School, she came up with constant surprises to lure historically truant youngsters back to school. She even said that she'd come to school in a gorilla suit if they all read a required number of books. They met the goal, and she kept her promise.
Act on a new idea as quickly as possible. Ideas have a short shelf life.	When The Nature Conservancy is notified that a parcel of land they wish to buy is available for purchase, they can get board approval and resources to place a down payment on the land within hours.
Seek innovative ideas from your customers.	In seeking to reinvent itself, the U.S. Forest Service conducted a series of town hall meetings designed to solicit

creative new ideas from those they serve.

Sustain innovation by paying for it.	The city of Phoenix's employee suggestion program pays an employee 10 percent (up to $2,500) of all savings attributed to his or her suggestion.
Take risks; focus on the positive.	"When people make mistakes," says Jesse Doyle, former executive director of the Spofford Detention Center run by New York City's Department of Juvenile Justice, "generally they don't do everything wrong. If there are ten steps in a process, most people get more than five right." At the DJJ they don't dwell on what people do wrong; they focus on what they do right. That way they can get the formula right and go forward to new horizons.

Form Effective Partnerships

Most of the organizations in this book have discovered that by joining forces with outside partners, they can leverage their efforts. In the most effective partnership arrangements, partners share equity, responsibility, and authority. Each partner is, in a true sense, a valued owner.

Make certain that each of your partners has a true sense of ownership. Recognize each contribution.	At Fairfax County's Medical Care for Children Project, partners meet regularly, update each other, and share new ideas and approaches. Recognition and credit are constantly passed around and made public. Each partner proudly refers to the project as "our project."
Establish partnerships that enable you to place your efforts closest to the action.	The Water Resources Division of the U.S. Geological Survey, charged with supplying the data necessary to ascertain the quantity and quality of the

nation's surface water supply, cannot effectively do its job alone. In partnership with more than 1,200 state and local agencies, the USGS obtains the manpower and skills it needs to meet its mission. In addition, the division benefits from the knowledge and experience of local officials and workers who understand the locale and the issues better than any Washington official possibly could.

Make sure that all partners are in for the long haul.

Partnership is the key to everything that The Nature Conservancy has accomplished overseas. The organization does everything it can to demonstrate to its Latin American partners that, through good times and bad, TNC will see any project through to completion.

Create win/win situations.

The partnership between the Wegmans food chain and the Rochester School District represents one of the most effective school/business collaborations in the nation. It's a true win/win situation. Through the partnership, Wegmans offers attractive incentives to youngsters who stay in school. In return, Wegmans gets not only valuable positive publicity but "first crack" at potentially valuable future employees.

Sell the Product

Fundraising is the lifeblood of most nonprofit organizations, and the nonprofits we've cited in this book have elevated fundraising to an art form. An ability to selling the product, however, is not confined to the nonprofits. Several of the government agencies we examined owe much of their successes to the ways in which they actively seek customers and promote their products and services.

Selling isn't a dirty word. It's a way of life.

The officials of the National Theatre Workshop of the Handicapped view every occasion as a sales possibility—cocktail parties, award ceremonies, class reunions. They identify potential donors through foundation books, business publications, and alumni magazines.

Know your buyer; tailor your pitch.

Before approaching any potential corporate buyer, the National Theatre Workshop of the Handicapped studies the corporation, analyzing its markets, goals, needs, and past donation history. The sales pitch is devised when the NTWH understands how supporting its organization can benefit a potential donor.

Make it easy for the customer to buy.

The Nature Conservancy offers potential donors a variety of ways in which they can contribute to the organization's coffers. Among other strategies, TNC created a planned giving program, an employer matching donation program, and a securities donation program.

Don't be afraid to be aggressive.

Seattle's Solid Waste Utility aggressively sells the idea of recycling to its citizen-customers. The utility sends direct mailings to customers, inserts information in utility bills, and publishes countless educational brochures. SWU staffers attend public meetings and conferences, man the phones to answer all customers' questions, and hold regular news conferences at which new programs and accomplishments are announced.

Communicate Effectively

Communication is the glue that holds organizations together. Every organization we visited emphasized the importance of communication. Every manager we talked to insisted that he or she didn't communicate enough, but the organizations we've cited do communicate constantly. They share ideas and concerns, good news and bad, achievements and failures. They have established cross-departmental teams, not only for efficiency's sake, but to open lines of communication between departments. Several have introduced courses in listening skills into their training programs.

Communicate by wandering around.	Four times a year, the commander of the Alameda Naval Aviation Depot staged a "walkaround." He traveled from one department to the next, making a presentation on the base's performance and projections for the months ahead. Nothing was held back.
Encourage everyone to share ideas and concerns. Listen to them.	Under the leadership of Ellen Schall and Rose Washington of New York City's Department of Juvenile Justice, no meeting was deemed a success unless everyone in the room had shared ideas and concerns and was truly listened to. Impromptu get-togethers as well as formal meetings were the mechanisms for communicating organizational issues.
Make it easy for people to communicate with the top.	Baltimore County's police chief created an open-door policy. Anyone at any level was free to walk in and discuss any issue with him.
Communicate constantly with your customers.	The success of Seattle's Solid Waste Utility is directly attributable to its passion for communicating with its customers in every form it can devise. Constant communication gains compliance, provides vital feedback, and leads to customer satisfaction.

Get the good news out.

Beth Israel Deaconess Medical Center understands that it is vital to let its people and the public know what the hospital is achieving. The medical center's extensive list of publications builds staff morale and customer and public support.

Minnesota's Department of Administration made sure that every opportunity for positive media and public recognition was seized upon. It operated under the philosophy that "positive press is the best hedge against bad times."

Our more than five years of observations and study have taught us that *all* of our main managerial concepts—focusing on mission, embracing change, managing for results, serving the customer, selling the product, creating effective partnerships, developing a climate for innovation, sharing the power, valuing people, and communicating effectively—build upon one another, and that the great majority of approaches and strategies we've presented are readily adaptable.

It's a safe bet to predict that you and the people around you are already practicing some of these strategies and approaches. Now we urge you to find ways to apply all of these ideas and adapt them for use throughout your organization. Remember, these strategies not only *can* be implemented; they *are* being implemented—and by people facing many of the same constraints and challenges that confront you. We know that you'll be pleased (and probably more than surprised) at the results.

INDEX